Out of the Crayon Box

Thoughts on Teaching, Retirement and Life

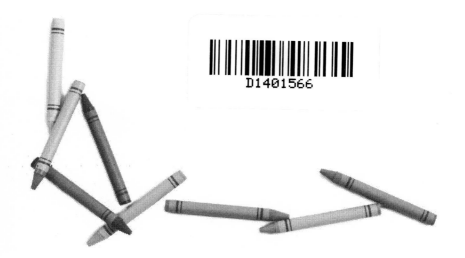

D1401566

By

Debra VanDeventer

Dedication

To my mother Alice, who encouraged me to go for it,
take a chance, and live my life to the fullest.

And to all past and present educators,
and the stories they hold in their hearts.

Table of Contents

Prologue
The End

It was hectic; the last days always were. A rainbow of acrylic colors stained my hands and the classroom sink, reminders of the fourth-grade rock painting activity. After completing their masterpieces, my students had arranged their personalized stones in the courtyard, a graduation tradition. As grown-up fifth graders next year, many will look back and think, *There's my rock! I was in that class!* Sticky tables were evidence of the artificially colored and flavored slushies a parent had brought in. The icy-neon concoctions we'd consumed with such glee were considered bad choices by the school's health code, but allowed today.

Contributing to the party mood, my co-teacher Lisa searched her computer for an appropriate soundtrack. Pre-adolescent bodies moved to the music, their energy fueled by a combination of anticipated summer freedom and the sugar rush provided by slushies. With just a few minutes left before dismissal, the students cajoled Lisa and me to join in. They burst into fits of laughter as their teachers tried to do "The Dab" and "The Floss." At the sound of the bell, students scrambled to stuff what remained of our nine months together into their bulging backpacks and raced out the door in a flurry of hugs and high fives.

1

Have a nice summer! Goodbye! Goodbye...

And so it was over, just like that. The room that had teemed with life and laughter moments before was quiet now. In a few days, I would experience relief and exhaustion from the busy year. One of my colleagues said it best, "Endings and beginnings take the most energy." With a sigh, I sank into my chair and fingered the card attached to the bouquet on my desk.

Dear Mrs. VanDeventer
Thank you so much for a wonderful year
And best wishes on your retirement!

There had been thirty-seven "last days" in my career as a teacher. This one signaled the end.

Part One

Breaking Up

(is hard to do)

Class Dismissed

How do you know when to retire? Maybe I'm not the best one to ask. I'm not very good at it. Out of three attempts to exit my teaching career, only one has been successful. The first time I seriously thought about leaving involved a pint-sized antagonist, assault with a deadly chair, and fleeing the classroom inwardly screaming, "I'm done! I can't take this anymore!" I wouldn't recommend going out this way.

I was twenty years into my teaching career when I first seriously considered ending it. The setting was a kindergarten room at Fodrea Community School, serving an economically disadvantaged area of Columbus, Indiana. Students who lived in this neighborhood often lacked the basic readiness skills, but they needed more than lessons in reading, writing, and math. My kindergarteners arrived in ill-fitting shoes and coats with broken zippers, dull hair and smudged noses, tired eyes and hungry tummies.

The psychological effects of poverty on their young lives were harder to see, but every bit as real. Many students lacked stability as they moved in and out of different schools several times a year, depending on which relative they were living with when the rent came due. They grew up street smart, knowing that if you didn't know how to fight, you wouldn't make it. The rules we taught differed from the rules they needed to survive their environment outside of the school walls, and this dichotomy often created chaos in the classroom.

One afternoon, I was working with a small group of struggling writers.

"I hate school!" Jared's shrill voice rang through the room. He clutched his pencil as he stared at the wide-lined paper, making no attempts to begin the writing assignment.

"It's OK. Let's try," I moved closer and knelt down beside my agitated student. We had been through this before. Coming from a home environment where books were rare and trips outside of the neighborhood were scarce had put Jared and many of his classmates at a disadvantage. Writing was hard, and rather than put in the effort to try, he typically balked. I was impatient to get the writing group back on task, frustrated that he had interrupted us once again. If I could just help him get the first few strokes on the page.

"You can't make me do this! This is stupid!" Jared exploded as he jumped up, sending the child-sized, plastic chair clattering to the floor behind him. I sprang to my feet, alarmed that things had escalated.

My heart pounded and my brain raced as I tried to figure out what to do.

"Whoa there, bud. Take it easy. I'll help you get started."

In an unexpected move, Jared grabbed the overturned chair and pointed the shiny, metal legs at me in defiance. The wide-eyed students in the writing group looked from me to their angry classmate. For a moment Jared and I stared at each other, locked in our own personal conflicts. Fight or flight? In a split second, my automatic response system sensed danger and chose "fight." My authority in the classroom was on the line. *Who does this little guy think he is? He's not in charge here, I am*, I thought as I wrenched the chair from my assailant and lurched towards him, ready for action. But in a decisive moment of self-preservation, my body intervened. *Get yourself out of this room NOW!* The command was as clear as if I'd shouted it out loud. A bundle of knotted nerves landed like a knife in my stomach. I doubled over. My teaching assistant, Danielle, rushed to my side.

"I need the nurse," I whispered from my folded position.

"Go!" she said with quiet urgency as she took my place in the writing center.

Not wanting to alarm my students, I held it together until I left the room. A volcano of sobs erupted as I entered the hallway; hot tears flowed down my cheeks. By the time I reached the office, I was hyperventilating. The startled nurse ushered me to the cot and had me breathe into a brown paper bag that smelled of peanut butter, as if someone had dumped their lunch to revive me. Our nurse was competent in bandaging scraped knees and checking for head lice. I had neither of these.

"Lie down," the nurse directed as she prepared to take my blood pressure.

By this time my principal, Joyce, heard the commotion and came dashing into the nurse's office.

"Deb, what's wrong? Tell me what happened!"

"We were writing...I...he...the chair... I didn't know what to do..." I sputtered as tears began again.

My head was spinning as I tried to make sense of what had happened. My colleagues knew me to be cool under fire, someone who could deal with pressure. Seeing me, a veteran teacher, in this condition alarmed the office staff. As I lay on the narrow vinyl-covered bed trying to compose myself, I imagined our commander-in-chief on her walkie-talkie announcing a bizarre emergency.

"Teacher down...I repeat TEACHER DOWN... We've lost Deb! The kindergarten students are taking over the school!"

The device strapped to my arm showed an alarmingly high blood pressure reading. When it had returned to a safer level, Joyce told me to take the rest of the day off and offered to drive me to the doctor's office. Embarrassed by the scene I had made, I assured her I could drive myself.

The sound of my careful footsteps echoed on the polished tile floors and projected a false sense of confidence as I walked back to the classroom. I dabbed at my wet, swollen eyes with a wadded up tissue, hoping to hide the traces of my meltdown. Danielle had Jared and the rest of the class under control. My students worried when they saw me grab my coat and purse from the closet. I told them I had a tummy ache and needed to go home. The story made sense to them. Many had seen me doubled over in pain, and they expressed their concern.

"I'll be fine," I reassured them. "Ms. Danielle will stay with you until the substitute teacher can get here. I'll see you tomorrow."

At the suggestion of the school nurse, I called my doctor and got an appointment for that afternoon. Driving across town, I wondered why I was so shaken. I replayed the scene in my mind once more: the writing assignment, the outburst, the chair. I was adept at handling difficult situations with patience. What was different this time? The awful truth washed over me. The situation wasn't unique; my reaction was. I was at my breaking point, acting out of anger, and on the verge of losing control. I could have broken down emotionally in front of the class or worse yet, I could have struck a child. That last thought terrified me and became the energy behind the pain that had caused me to double over, ensuring that I left the room before I slipped over the edge.

The doctor diagnosed an anxiety attack brought on by exhaustion and stress, and recommended I take some time off. She suggested the usual stress management options such as yoga, meditation, diet, and exercise. Then she asked if I might consider changing careers.

I was tempted to end it right there. I was still young enough to switch careers. There were plenty of jobs out there where I could make more money with less stress. For the rest of the afternoon I sat on my living room sofa and did some soul searching. Was I ready to throw in the towel? With a master's degree and twenty years' experience I had a lot invested in my career. I liked the staff I was currently working with and I was making progress with this little group of kindergarteners. I couldn't leave them now.

Deciding it wasn't time to retire from teaching, I realized I needed to make some changes. Taking the doctor's advice, I found a way to arrange my schedule that year so I had enough time to drive home for lunch. After eating, I would set the timer and lie down on the living room floor for a few minutes to breathe deeply and relax. It got me through the rest of the year. Maybe I became numb to the stress, but I'd like to think as I became more skilled, I learned to handle it better. I honed my planning skills by learning to be prepared to expect the unexpected. Along with other staff members, I participated in specialized training to find ways to meet the educational and emotional needs of economically disadvantaged students. My experiences at Fodrea made me a stronger teacher and created opportunities to move into a variety of teaching and educational consulting positions that extended my career.

It would be many years before I considered retiring again. This time it was a numbers game. Like most teachers, I did the math. To retire with a full pension, one you had been contributing to since your first paycheck, you need to arrive at a predetermined score. This varies from state to state, but the formula goes something like this: your age, plus the number of years taught, minus the number of teacher mugs in your possession, divided by the number of sturdy shoes in your closet. You get bonus points if your hair has turned prematurely gray. This magic number is your golden ticket to leave the classroom, if you choose, and enter the "Willy Wonka" land of retirement delights.

At the age of sixty-two, with thirty-four years of teaching behind me, I surpassed my magic number and announced my first official retirement. My husband Ed had already retired from teaching high school and was waiting for me to follow suit. We planned carefully as we sold our home in Indiana and purchased a house in the Southwest. But something funny happened on the way to Arizona. Though my numbers added up, I realized I wasn't ready to retire. It's hard to explain, but I had the feeling that there was more to come. Even as I packed boxes, I sent out my resume to school districts in Tucson.

I kept this to myself, not telling Ed until I received a request for an interview. At first he wasn't happy. This didn't fit into our master plan. We had plans to travel and enjoy our new home in Tucson. After talking it over, we agreed I would give it a trial run for one year. The state of Arizona granted me a three year teaching certificate and, based on my experience and qualifications, I wouldn't have to take additional classes or pass any qualifying tests. Though my pay was a fraction of what I'd been earning, I would be able to collect my Indiana pension and my new contract included health care for Ed and myself. I was at peace with my decision as I accepted the fourth grade position, but this made for awkward conversations at my retirement party in the library of Rock Creek Elementary School in Columbus, Indiana.

"Congratulations! I am so happy for you! Now you can take it easy."

"Well, see... I... um... I'm not *really* retiring... I just... um... accepted a fourth grade teaching position... in Tucson... Arizona..." I mumbled.

The pleasant chatter in the room stopped, the festive helium balloons deflated, and mouths dropped open in astonishment. Teachers rarely say this while drinking punch and eating snacks at their retirement celebration. I imagined my colleagues might scrape my name off the decorated cake and take back their gifts as they made their way to the door, sorry they'd wasted their time and money on me. No one did, but I'm sure they thought I had lost my mind.

My "trial year" of teaching in Tucson lasted three years. I'll admit it wasn't easy to start over in a new state and a new grade level. Part of me bristled at my "Year One" designation and the extra hours I put into the beginning teacher program the district assigned me to. But another part of me, the better part, embraced the challenge. I considered myself a poster child for experienced teachers who had the guts to try something new. My slogan became "Old enough for Social Security, young enough to be a first-year teacher."

I made lasting friendships during this encore period, and at times I wanted to go on forever. I kept current with the ever-changing technology and curriculum demands, but it was getting harder to maintain my energy level and patience. The title of a book from one of my college courses came to mind: *The Geranium on the Windowsill Just Died, But Teacher, You Kept Right on Going.* I didn't want to fade away like a tired old plant in the window. I wanted to go out as a vibrant contributor to my profession.

That was the example my father had set. Our retirement stories bore similarities. Dad retired reluctantly at sixty-five, the mandatory retirement age for deans at Indiana University. They kept him on as an honorary professor. Dad had always been career centered, being most comfortable when he was in his professional world. I went to visit him in his new office one day after his retirement. No longer in charge and with no real work to do, he looked like a lost puppy. Within six months, slightly longer than *my* first retirement, he'd accepted a position as an interim dean at a college in Missouri. When he announced this to the family, he intended for this to be temporary. As soon as the college secured a permanent dean, he would retire. Then he could travel with Mom, write his book, and spend time with his children and grandchildren. Before any of these things happened, my father died. I was heartbroken. We had no way of knowing that his life would end suddenly, but I felt cheated out of the chance to get to know him outside of his professional persona. He left behind unfulfilled dreams.

How do you know when it's time to retire? It's a personal question I had to figure out for myself. I won't deny that my father's early death had an impact. I would soon be the age he was when he died and wanted to do the things he never got to do: travel, write a book, and spend time with my children and grandchildren.

When the day came to make it official, I hesitated just a moment, then placed my letter of intent to retire on the principal's desk at Manzanita Elementary. This time the single sheet of paper felt solid, weighty, and permanent. Though I didn't yet have a clear picture of what the next chapter of my life would look like, I knew it was time for it to begin.

Curtain Call

"And this year's retiring teacher is..."

I stand as the announcer calls my name, and I smooth out my star-studded evening gown. The crowd claps and cheers. Through the dim lights, I recognize the faces of my colleagues seated around the elaborate ballroom, raising their champagne glasses to toast this milestone occasion. I approach the stage...

The rasp of the lunch bell jarred me out of my Cinderella fantasy. My gown dissolved into jeans and a staff T-shirt, and the ballroom turned back into the school cafeteria.

Just yesterday this space teemed with high-spirited first and second graders. Their excited chatter crashed through the room heralding the last day of school. Wafts of pepperoni pizza and hamburgers bounced off the fluorescent lights and lingered in the air. Remains of neglected lunches littered the tables, and the floors were sprinkled with napkins and straw-wrapper confetti as the custodian tried to keep up. Teacher assistants monitored the place like weary border collies, trying their best to summon enough energy and patience to make it through a few more hours, or at least until the bell dismissed their charges for the final recess of the year.

A different scene greeted me today. Instead of students, adults sat at the lunch tables. A pleasant hum filled the air as snippets of conversation floated by. Freshly mopped floors hinted of disinfectant, and the scrubbed table tops showed no evidence of ketchup and mustard wars. Though not the formal ballroom of my fantasy retirement celebration, the social committee had decorated the space with bouquets and streamers to create a festive mood for this traditional luncheon. It was the end of the school year for my colleagues. The end of a career for me.

Lured by the aroma of the catered meal, I walked towards the buffet. I picked up my paper plate and plastic silverware and joined my friends filling their plates with pasta, salad, and breadsticks.

"Deb! Sit over there. We've saved a place for you close to the stage," my teammate Claire pointed to a spot near the front of the room then bounded away, her long dark hair bouncing behind her. I smiled fondly at the young, energetic teacher I'd mentored a year ago.

"I'll be right there!" I replied as I pushed the salad to one side of my plate to make room for a scoop of lasagna.

An elaborately decorated cake was displayed on the dessert table. The word *CONGRATULATIONS* was written in royal blue across the smooth white frosting and the names of the retirees were spelled out in red icing. This was the second time in my career I'd seen my name on a retirement cake. I was still staring at it when Melanie, one of the other retirees, walked by.

"We'd better get a piece of our cake before it's gone. I want one with my name on it," she said. "I heard they've already started interviewing to fill our positions."

"Ha! They didn't waste any time," I faked a laugh and walked on, not wanting to cut my name out of the center of the cake. A familiar knot began to form in the pit of my stomach. I wondered how long it would take before Retirement Anxiety grabbed me this time. Shaking it off, I headed to the table to join my teammates.

After setting my loaded plate on the cafeteria table, I eased myself onto the attached stool. Having the time to sit and enjoy lunch in the company of friends was a luxury. On a normal school day I'd be in my room alone, washing down a sandwich with swigs of Diet Coke while answering emails or preparing for afternoon classes.

"So are you done with report cards?" Denise asked. She was the creative spark on our team, always coming up with new ideas to try. Denise was one of those teachers who liked to go with the flow and use student ideas to drive the curriculum. That's how she worked best. Sticking to a strict timeline was not her style and report cards were her nemesis. I knew she would be working non-stop to meet the deadline. I couldn't resist the tease.

"Didn't you know that retiring teachers get to skip report cards?" I joked. "No, seriously, they won't let me leave until they're done. The grades are recorded and I've been working all morning on adding comments. Hopefully I'll have them finished soon, then on to some serious packing."

"Just think..." Lisa smiled. "These are the last report cards you'll ever do. It must be nice."

"Yep, it is!" I agreed.

Filling out report cards was one thing I would *not* miss. I could add recess supervision, and cafeteria duty to that list as well as stress, fatigue, and anxiety. Teaching is arduous work, and the demands on teachers seemed to increase every year. I'd stuck with it longer than most, having postponed my exit for three years when I moved to Arizona. This time it was official. My retirement paperwork was on the principal's desk, and the smiling faces and party atmosphere in the lunchroom confirmed it. Even the cake was congratulating me.

Yet, I would miss some things. I had worked alongside some of the most talented and interesting people in education. The three sitting with me were no exception, and we had developed a close friendship. I felt like I was breaking up a long-term relationship. Lisa and I had become especially close this year as we had embarked on a team-teaching arrangement, combining both of our classes and sharing the teaching responsibilities. "We can still be friends," she'd said when I announced my retirement. Nevertheless, I knew it wouldn't be the same.

That was my real fear. Nothing would be the same. Teaching had been my work and my world for thirty-seven years. Would I know how to do anything else? Could I adjust to the world outside of the crayon box? This thought ping-ponged around my brain as I tried to engage in conversations at the table. Just minutes away from my presentation, the magnitude of my decision sunk in. *Well, it's too late to change your mind now,* I told myself. My stomach churned, and I picked at my lunch.

As the social committee moved on to the business portion of the event, my anxiety mounted. Several employees were being honored: some retiring, some moving on to pursue other interests. I was doing both, though I'd yet to figure out what those other interests might be. The program included a lovely speech by a teacher assistant who wanted to spend time with her newborn grandchild. Another faculty member had decided to move to a different state. Her beautiful video presentation brought many to tears. Thankfully, my own watery eyes wouldn't stand out.

When the social committee chairman announced my name, I made my way to the front of the room along with my fourth-grade teaching team. My three teammates took turns making gracious comments while handing me some clever beach-themed gifts. An inflatable life ring (to remind me I'd helped them stay afloat), goggles (I had the ability to see situations clearly), and diving toys (I'd encouraged them to dive deeper into the curriculum). After a heart-felt group hug, my friends returned to their seats.

It was my turn to speak. The audience sat politely, but they had listened to several presentations already and had much work to do in their classrooms. Besides, the child-sized, lunch-table stools were getting uncomfortable and making dents in adult backsides. I had an excellent excuse to keep it short. Many speeches ran through my head. How could I capture my extensive career in a few words? How would I sum up the hundreds of students and colleagues who had touched my heart and continued to mean so much? I'd always taken pride in my public-speaking ability and was comfortable in front of large groups; now words escaped me. Why hadn't I created a cute video or at least written a few notes in preparation?

All eyes turned to me and the silence hung heavy in the air as I swallowed a lump in my throat. After composing myself, I uttered a few phrases of thanks, expressing it was time to pass the torch and that I would leave the future of education in expert hands. Applause signaled the conclusion of the day's speeches and I returned to my little stool at the table. I was relieved to be out of the spotlight, yet I knew I had not delivered the speech that was in my heart. The principal made a few end-of-year announcements and dismissed us.

Dismissed. As everyone scurried to their classrooms or offices to work, I hung back. That's when it hit me—I was retired. It was official this time. The line I'd just stepped over was as obvious as if I had drawn it with a marker on the lunchroom floor. Thick and permanent. I was different now. They were teachers, I was not. They were teammates, I was going solo. They were packing their room for the summer; I was shutting that door forever.

On the way out, I passed the dessert table. The celebration cake had been reduced to a few edge pieces set out on paper plates. Chocolate crumbs and blobs of white icing smeared the doily-lined cardboard tray. I picked up one of the remaining pieces of cake to take back to my room. Afraid I couldn't plaster another smile on my face, I avoided the main hallway. The less traveled, open-air walkway that wandered past the kindergarten rooms was my favorite part of the campus. I'd fallen in love with this space when the principal introduced me to the school three years ago. The Arizona sunshine filtered through the branches of the palo verde trees and made lacy patterns on the sidewalk.

I sat on the stairway by the outdoor dining pavilion. It was quiet. Was it only yesterday that Jack and Andrew were trying to see who could chug their milk and make the loudest belch? Wasn't it Gordon who missed the trash can as he was trying to dump the rest of his sandwich out of his lunchbox so his mom would think he'd finished his lunch? It had to have been Kia, Megan, and Lilly who were singing the latest Britney Spears song at the top of their lungs while the boys at the next table clutched their hearts and pretended to swoon. Then there was the chaos that erupted as a hundred fourth graders scrambled to pitch what was left of their lunches and lined up for the last recess of the year. *Ha! No cafeteria or playground duty for me today... or tomorrow... or ever. I'm retired. This is what I wanted... It's going to be great... right?*

The little square of cake on the festive paper plate mocked me. A squiggle of blue icing was all that remained of the word "Congratulations!" *Congratulations.* This was a day to celebrate a job well done, and look forward to some much needed rest and relaxation. So why the tears? I'd been betrayed. Through all the retirement seminars and talks with friends who had left the profession before me, nobody had told me it was going to hurt. Would it feel like ripping a Band-Aid off, one serious *ouch* and I'd be over it, or would the pain linger, perhaps fading away in bits and pieces?

I was about to find out. I headed back to my classroom to finish packing up a considerable chunk of my life.

Out on the Curb

It was a daunting task. For several days, my life was a mess of boxes and packing tape as I attempted to dismantle my teaching life. Down to the last bits, I'd come in early to finish. The room was stuffy and warm. My hands were grimy from dust that had accumulated on items I'd found in nooks and crannies. I grabbed a diet soda from the mini fridge and held the can to my forehead before popping it open. The cold, bubbly liquid refreshed me as I took a satisfying swig, expecting the caffeine to kick in soon and give me the jolt I needed.

"Knock, knock!" Carol, the fifth grade teacher down the hall startled me. "Wow! It looks like you're about done!"

"Yeah, I got an early start this morning. I set these aside for you." I pointed to the corner of the room.

In my last three years, my "encore career" in Arizona, I'd been trying out new ideas in the classroom to keep myself energized. When mindfulness training for teachers and students became a topic of focus, I was motivated to create a tranquil corner. Carol had come to pick up some items so she could set up her own space next year.

"I'm afraid I gave away my tub of kinetic sand," I apologized. "Dominic enjoyed it so much, I sent it home with him on the last day of school. I sealed the box with a double layer of tape and warned him not to open it until he got home. It was great for kids who needed extra tactile input. You should get some for your Mindfulness corner."

"I'll see if I'm brave enough. I'd better let you get on with your packing. Will we see you next year? Are you going to sub or volunteer?" Carol said as she lugged the beanbag chair and basket of relaxing music CDs to the door.

"No, I think I'm done."

"Well, let me know if you change your mind. Good subs are hard to find. We'd keep you busy around here!"

"That's what I'm afraid of!" I joked.

Alone again, I took stock of what was left to be done. A few hints of my teaching style remained scattered throughout the space. Yoga-ball chairs, now deflated and boxed, were a reminder of my experiment with flexible seating options. The philosophy behind this idea was that students would benefit if they had a choice of where to sit in the classroom. Curious about this, I had outfitted my room with tables for groups, tall stools and a bar height table for pairs of students or teacher check-ins, and individual study pods along the counter for privacy. The reading nook with its area rug, sling chair, and floor lamp had been a popular spot to hang out with a favorite book.

My fourth graders were enthusiastic about the flexible seating in the room, and it had worked well... with one exception. In theory, perching on a yoga ball instead of a traditional seat would benefit those who needed to move around. I'd done my research, purchased three chairs, and had prepared the class with expectations for the use of the novel seats, including a schedule for taking turns.

On the first morning, things seemed to be working out nicely. Then Devon got up to sharpen his pencil and his "seat" rolled away. The class giggled. I hadn't thought to purchase the stabilizing rings that would keep the chairs in place. We spent much of that first day retrieving run-away yoga balls.

The next day, it was Dominic's turn. This little guy was a whirlwind of activity. I was confident the yoga chair would allow him the movement he needed. Evidently, he "needed" more movement than I could handle. First a small bounce, not more than a hiccup really, then the bounces became higher and higher. Soon the occupants of the other two yoga ball chairs began to bounce. It became a game to see who could bounce the highest and still stay out of trouble. The sight of bouncing bodies drove me *crazy*.

Sit still! I wanted to scream. I'd introduced the yoga balls into the room to allow for movement, but this was too much. As the day wore on I established a

"Your-behind-can't-bounce-over-five-inches-off-the-chair-rule" which was of course, impossible to enforce. The chairs were out of control. The experience was a wake-up call for me. There was a time in my career when I would have had the patience to work through some solutions while enjoying the challenge of problem solving, but I was over it. Maybe it was a sign that I was near the end. By the third day, I'd deflated the chairs and ended my experiment, placing the rolling rovers in storage.

When it came time to clear out my room for the last time I sent a staff email:

Three yoga-ball chairs, gently used.
Free to a good home.

Mark responded first and had already carried them back to his fifth grade room. I didn't tell him about the bouncing butts. He'd figure it out for himself. I'd already hauled off the rest of the "flexible seating" furniture pieces to the Goodwill store, also known as "Classroom Decor and More," where most of it came from. That took care of the big items in the room.

Moving to the bookshelf, I packed a collection of stuffed animals and children's books. One of my teammates was teaching kindergarten next year, and these would make an impressive addition to her library. As I put each book and character in the box, it brought back fond memories of sitting in front of a group of students sharing my favorite stories. Wiggly bodies calmed and classroom walls evaporated as words transported us to times, places, and emotions we might never reach on our own. Before sealing the box, I included a note that Claire would find when she unpacked: Take good care of my friends.

As I ripped a large strip of tape from the dispenser, I glimpsed the furry, yellow face of the Star-Bellied Sneetch peeking up at me. At the last minute, I plucked it and the matching book out of the box. I couldn't bear to leave him; we'd been through a lot together. Though one of Seuss' lesser known stories, "The Sneetches," was a favorite read aloud of mine. In typical Seuss-style the story was rhythmic and fun to read aloud. Using the silly Sneetches, some star bellied, some plain, Dr. Seuss tells a story of inclusiveness. For Dr. Seuss day, I dressed the part, concocting a costume out of a thrift store yellow knit dress that I embellished with an enormous green star on the "belly" and a feather-boa collar. With bright green tights and rubber gloves I wore on my feet to mimic bird legs, I made my grand entrance, greeted by squeals of laughter. I would gather my cluster of kiddos and begin:

Now the Star-Belly Sneetches had bellies with stars...

I placed the book, stuffed animal, and costume in the box labeled KEEP, just in case I ever got called back into action. You never know when someone might need a Sneetch.

When I had finished packing, the room looked as it had the first day I'd seen it — bare bulletin boards, tables and chairs pushed against the walls, books and materials packed away. Devoid of life. The space was now a blank slate, ready for next year's teacher to weave his or her magic. In my retirement speech, I said I would be passing the torch to my fellow educators. Little did I know my "torch" would be a bean bag chair, yoga balls, and a collection of stuffed animals. I was hoping to bequeath decades of experience and a bit of my teaching spirit as well.

With a quick look around, I picked up my last box, locked the door, and made my way to the office. It had been a difficult, yet therapeutic process. I was closing this chapter of my life and moving on.

"Well, that's that," I said as I handed my keys to Joan, the administrative assistant.

"Oh... gosh... we're going to miss you..."

"Me too," was all I could say. A few tears escaped my eyes as she came out from behind the desk to give me a hug.

"Come back and see us!"

"I will," I promised, yet I knew in my heart it wouldn't be the same.

As I headed to the car with my last box, it reminded me of a scene often played out in films where security guards escort a terminated office worker out of the building. In the movies, they leave the employee sitting on the curb with a carton of belongings as she wonders where to go and what to do next. In my real-life exit from teaching, there were no guards, no one had forced me to go, and my car was full of many boxes. I did, however, sympathize with the movie character in one regard. I had no idea where to go from here.

My friend called from across the parking lot. "I'm so jealous! I have several years to go before I can retire, but I'm already thinking of what I want to do when the time comes. Have a great summer!"

"Thanks, you too!" I stuffed the overflowing box in the backseat and slid into the oven-like interior of my sixteen-year-old Saturn, hoping the air conditioner would kick in soon.

The car was full with what I wanted to keep, children's books and mementos of my last few years of teaching. There was a large stack of teacher assessments and paperwork that I wasn't sure what to do with. It was a relief to have this behind me. I'd said goodbye to my room, my friends, and my career. With a sigh, I glanced in the rearview mirror as I drove out of the parking lot and turned towards home. Just a few weeks ago, I'd seen a prophetic sign at the hairdresser's, of all places:

Don't look back... You're not going that way.

As Manzanita Elementary faded into the background that afternoon, there was a small but significant shift in my disposition. I felt lighter than I had in years as a sense of freedom enveloped me. I was on my way to a new adventure! And yet, my friend's words lingered in my mind. She had already been looking ahead to retirement. For the moment, my plans consisted of getting this stuff home and sleeping in tomorrow morning. Panic set in as I realized I didn't have a solid plan for this next stage. I had a general sense that I wouldn't be spending ten hours of my day in school. Weekends and summers would be free of paper grading and curriculum planning. But what *would* I do? I'd created a space for myself in the crayon box world and had been secure in my role. Would I be able to adjust to living "on the outside?"

Several days after my massive move from the classroom, I was still thinking about this. Undaunted, I did what any self-respecting teacher does when trying to come up with a strategy. My technology skills were up to date and my fingers were nimble from years of zipping jackets and tying shoes. I opened my computer and looked for resources. Scores of educators had gone before me; surely someone had left a guidebook, some notes, or at least a breadcrumb trail to the Gingerbread Home for Recently Retired Teachers.

My search proved disappointing. Most of my efforts lead to books or articles that dealt with the financial planning aspect of retirement, such as *How to Retire to Columbia... Comprehensive Guide from an Expat*. Perhaps I could leave the country before any disgruntled students or parents found me, but this seemed a bit drastic. Then I found *How to Generate Real Estate Streams to Supplement your Retirement*. I wasn't interested in real estate streams; it was hard enough to keep track of one home.

This title caught my eye: *Funny Retirement Notebook for Teachers*. The cover was cute; however, when I clicked to look inside, the pages were plain lined notebook pages... not funny, and not what I was hoping to find. It was a "do-it-yourself" journal. I was looking for a step-by-step guide where someone had worked out the kinks and pitfalls of retirement. Besides, I needed some help in dealing with the conflicting emotions I was feeling. That's when I found *The Dr. Seuss Meditation Coloring Book* under the category of "resources for retired teachers."Well now, here is something I can do with my time. I like to color, and it might be relaxing. "One fish... two fish... redfish... bluefish..." At least I wouldn't have to decide on what color to make the fish. I wonder if it includes red and blue crayons.

My search went nowhere. Though I'd spent countless hours and thousands of dollars preparing to enter the field of education, there seemed to be few if any resources to help me leave a career that had spanned decades. Some teachers plan a graceful exit, weaning themselves off gradually by substituting or teaching part time. For me, it was an abrupt ending. As a host of a popular TV reality program says when a contestant gets voted off the show, "One day you're in, the next day... you're OUT."

I clicked off the computer and stared at the blank screen. It appeared I would be sitting on the curb for a while to figure things out.

Adjustment. Period.

It's embarrassing to admit, but the first thing I did when I retired was fall asleep. I don't mean sleeping a little, this was hibernation. I left the bed or couch only to forage for food. The woman who had dressed with care each morning, donning her name-tag lanyard with pride, was now spending her days in the same yoga pants and an oversized T-shirt. This dormant period went on for weeks. I thought there was something physically or mentally wrong with me.

This was problematic because I come from a family that values hard work and achievement. My father, Jack, dedicated himself to his profession. He was respected in his field, not only for his expertise but also for his leadership abilities. He had been a dean at three universities during his career. Dad liked to have his life organized. He kept a small appointment book in his pocket at all times. If I ever needed a sharpened pencil, ruler, or stapler for a school project, I was sure to find what I needed in one of his tidy desk drawers.

My mother, Alice, grew up in the 1930s in the middle of a pack of thirteen children. She believed you could get anywhere you wanted to go in life if you worked hard enough. As a teenager, she left home to work for a wealthy family in town. They provided room and board and a meager salary in exchange for babysitting and housework she did on the weekends and after school. In today's world, we would consider this child labor, but instead of complaining, my mother saw this as an opportunity to better herself. After marrying and having children, Mom embodied the stereotypical 1950s stay-at-home-mom, working hard to make sure her four children had the home that she dreamed of as a child. She immersed herself into any task she tackled whether decorating, sewing, refinishing furniture, hosting parties, or heading up social committees.

Mom's creativity manifested itself during holidays. Our Halloween costumes were always over the top. Once, she fashioned a horse costume for my brother and I. She constructed the body from cardboard boxes supported by a broom handle. Then we draped a sheet over this frame, added a paper horse-head mask, and finished the whole contraption with a yarn tail. I was the horse's head while my younger brother was the horse's... well, you get the idea. Another time, Mom used RITZ dye tablets in our washing machine to turn old bed sheets into a green dragon large enough to cover four kids. For months, our clothes had a slight olive tinge after coming through the wash. And don't get me started on the extent to which she ramped up for Christmas.

If one of Mom's projects was underway, it often took over the whole house. When this happened, Dad retreated to the safety of his well-ordered home office or left the house to catch up on work at the university. This worked for my parents, and I used this dichotomy of role models to my advantage. I like to think the combination of Dad's professionalism and order, and Mom's crazy creativity came together to prepare me for my life as an elementary school teacher. Sometimes I'm Jack, often I'm Alice. Either way, I am wired for productivity.

This was the source of my anxiety. Although Dad nodded off after dinner occasionally, Mom never slowed down. After I retired, she expressed her views on work and sleeping during a phone conversation.

"How are you? Are you working?"

"No Mom, I'm retired."

"Well what are you doing?"

"Sleeping."

"Oh... my. You should do *something.*"

Maybe mom was right, I thought as I glanced at my yoga pants. I should do something. I got off the sofa and began to pace around the house, stressing over my lack of motivation. My husband, Ed, put this in perspective for me.

"Don't worry about it," he said. "You've been working hard and running on adrenaline for a long time. Obviously your body needs rest."

That's why I love this guy. He's often the one who helps me take a step back when I'm in Alice mode. He was right; after years of teaching I needed time to unwind. I decided not to be too concerned.

But now I had lots of free time and I wasn't sure how to fill my days. As a teacher, I was used to dividing each day into neat little boxes in my plan book. The school schedule fit together like a giant jigsaw puzzle. Once the master agenda fell into place, I arranged my daily schedule around it. Out of necessity, I had become an expert in the art of time management. I was proud of my ability to plan each day to the fullest, and I clung to the little boxes in my plan book as if my life depended on them.

Having been in a school setting since I was five years old, the ebb and flow of the school year was second nature to me. In the classroom, I knew what day it was. The agenda and decorated calendar on the bulletin board made it easy to pinpoint where I stood in the space-time continuum. It was like the big maps you see in public places with the arrow that says YOU ARE HERE. Now, the arrow had disappeared. I was losing track of days. Seasons and holidays snuck up on me without warning.

And here's another weird thing. I swear, I had to go through potty training again. I don't mean I needed adult diapers (I'm sure that will come along soon enough) but it seemed strange that I could go to the bathroom when needed. In a school setting, I scheduled even this basic biological function. The whole class lined up and proceeded down the hallway to the bathroom for scheduled bathroom breaks. This was when my students were supposed to go, on demand. Heaven forbid if the urge struck someone at an unscheduled time. Of course, the student would be allowed to go, but she or he would have to get permission, sign out, and take along an embarrassingly gigantic BATHROOM PASS, announcing to the world that they had not planned accordingly.

Unable to leave my class unsupervised, I would schedule my personal bathroom time when the class was out of the room. On some days my first break might be lunch time. Early in my teaching career, I learned how to gauge my input/output ratio. It was best not to stop by the coffee shop or drink that extra cup of tea on my way to school. If I miscalculated my intake, I would need to have my assistant or the teacher next door take over the class while I dashed to the bathroom in the teacher's lounge. In a worst-case scenario, I might have to use the tiny kindergarten toilets in my room. These were often smelly and messy as a result of five-year-old boys who had not yet perfected their aim.

Now that I wasn't on a set schedule, my bladder was confused. After years of deferring to my brain to say when it was OK to go, it was trying to regain a sense of control. At first I was peeing every hour. It took a while for my brain and bladder to communicate again. Brain promised Bladder it wouldn't have to wait until lunchtime; they worked out a comfortable agreement.

Then, there was the lunch situation. I was now free to eat anytime and didn't have to worry about having cafeteria duty, but how long would it take before I realized I had more than ten minutes to gulp down a sandwich and chug a diet Coke? It was embarrassing to go to lunch with new (non-teacher) friends and be the first one finished.

And it was strange to be able to roam freely throughout the day. One afternoon, early in my retirement, I stopped by Starbucks. I remember thinking *Wow! I'm at Starbucks in the middle of the day!* The softly lit room smelled of roasting coffee and soothing music played in the back-ground. I picked up my latte and sank into an overstuffed chair, aware that I was in no hurry to go anywhere. It was a stark contrast to the world of teaching. I felt like I had entered a new dimension.

As discreetly as possible, I began to observe my fellow coffee shop patrons. Who were these people who could go to Starbucks at two o'clock on a Tuesday afternoon? Two young women were chatting while a baby snoozed in a car seat on the bench between them. A group of spandex-clad seniors shared a laugh on the patio next to their safely secured bicycles. At a nearby table, a businesswoman was working simultaneously on her phone and her laptop. A small group appeared to be discussing a book.

Where did I fit in?

My identity as a professional woman was packed away in a box in my closet with an assortment of name tags that reflected positions I held through the years: preschool teacher, kindergarten teacher, first grade teacher, teacher coach, keynote speaker, learning facilitator, fourth grade teacher, and instructional consultant.

Who was I now?

RETIRED. This is how I would identify myself in the "occupation" section on official forms from now on.

How would I live out this new identity?

True to Jack and Alice, I had worked hard. Besides my career, I maintained a strong marriage and raised a family.

Now what?

I took the last sip of my now lukewarm latte and glanced around the coffee shop once more before heading to my car. Yes, this would be an adjustment. Period. I pledged to allow myself an entire year, a sabbatical if you will, where I would resist the urge to jump into any major commitments. I needed time to reset my brain before I could move on.

Plays Well With Others

They warned me.

"You will get through your first summer," retired teachers said, "but watch out for the start of the new school year. That's when it hits you."

I didn't get it until the back-to-school ads appeared in the newspaper. Restlessness set in. I began to wake early and pace through the days in anticipation. In anticipation of what?

The realization dawned on me slowly. Of course... I was preparing for the New Year. On the school calendar, the clock I'd been synced to for most of my life, New Year's Day wasn't celebrated on the first of January. The New Year started on the first day of school and ended on the last day in May or early June. The school-calendar clock was still ticking in my soul. The New Year was coming.

There is an excitement that builds at the beginning of a new school year. I remember my mother taking me to get school supplies when I was a child, maybe some new clothes and shoes as well. I was searching for the supplies that would carry me to academic excellence, or at least make me look like one of the cool kids.

When I was in fourth grade it was the Nifty Notebook. This notebook was so cool that the word "nifty" was part of its official name, thus eliminating any doubt about its coolness. The Nifty Notebook was sleek compared to its clunky cousin the three-ring binder. No longer would you need to lug around that large, denim-covered beast that pinched your fingers with a loud snap every time you tried to add or remove a piece of paper.

The Nifty Notebook was a product of the Mod 1960s. It came in a variety of neon-colored vinyl covers, not unlike the fashion icons of the day. It was a radical rule breaker, requiring the purchase of special paper designed with two holes punched at the top. But the thing that really made the Nifty stand out was its state-of-the-art technology. Two posts held the paper in place and when you folded the slim plastic top down the hidden magnets engaged with a soft click. Deluxe models included a built-in pencil case in the top.

Eventually, the Nifty Notebook went out of vogue, ending up in the back of the closet along with my go-go boots. I grew up, went to college, and became a teacher. This choice of career allowed me to continue my passion for school supplies, and my giddiness about the first day of school renewed itself each year.

As a teacher, I loved getting my room ready. I convinced myself that the right combination of room arrangement and color-coordinated organizational gadgets would start the year off right. My energy level peaked in the weeks before school started as I moved tables and chairs around, set up the fish aquarium, and prepared eye-catching bulletin boards. I sent out letters welcoming my new students and took pride in putting their names on tables and cubbies. Like a marathon runner, I burst out of the starting gate with a well-organized room, eager to meet and greet my new class.

I was beginning to understand what the words "watch out for the end of summer" meant. My energy rush was building on cue as it had for so many years, but now it had nowhere to go. Thinking I could get my 'back-to-school' fix, I had lunch with my teacher friends before they returned to their classrooms. They were busy and stressed as they rushed to get things ready. I felt left out.

"Boy, I'll bet you're glad you are not doing this!" they said.

"It will be so nice. You can sleep in and do whatever you want!"

"Yeah!" I agreed. "It will be great!"

But I wasn't so sure. Back home, I tried to keep busy. I filled my days with reading and small projects around the house.

A few days later, Ed and I were at Target when my cart veered into the dollar section at the front of the store. I froze. Dr. Seuss pencils, Welcome Back banners, calendars, pencil cups, plastic totes, color-coordinated planners, notebooks, and file folders shouted *"Pick me! Pick me!"* Imagine the possibilities! Ed, noticing that I was no longer behind him, traced his steps back and found me staring at the display.

"What are you doing here?" he asked.

"Look... pencils... two packs for a dollar, and look at those notebooks!"

"Deb, you don't need those this year. Remember? You don't have a class anymore."

He put his arm on my shoulder and guided me away with a worried look on his face. I glanced back to see a half a dozen teachers filling their carts with school supplies. They had giddy looks on their faces as if they had won the lottery. One of them was talking into her cell phone.

"Jen! I'm here at Target and they have those cute pencil cans we can use on our tables! Three for a dollar! Do we want the solid blue ones or the ones with the colorful polka dots? Here, let me send you a picture. They won't last long!"

"Go with the polka dots!" I wanted to say, *"You can't go wrong with polka dots... and get the matching notebooks, too!"* But there would be no polka dot pencil cans for me this year. I trudged through the store on a boring quest for toilet tissue.

One night, long after Ed had gone to bed, I sat on the sofa feeling sorry for myself and wondering if I had made the right decision. *Maybe I'm one of those people who isn't happy being retired,* I thought. Tears began to trickle, and I needed to talk to someone. I shuffled into the bedroom and flopped onto the bed with a sigh. No response from my sleeping husband, so I jiggled the bed and exaggerated my sigh. Ed propped himself up on one arm and squinted at the clock.

"What are you doing up so late?"

"I'm not happy!"

"What?"

"I have nothing to do... and all my friends are working!" I whined in my most pitiful voice hoping to elicit a sympathetic response.

"Well, call the school and get your job back!" Ed grumbled. He rolled over and went back to sleep.

I love this man, but he wasn't the understanding girlfriend I needed at the moment. After drying my tears on my pillow I eventually fell asleep. When my principal called a few days later and offered me a full-time subbing position, I reaffirmed that I didn't want my teaching job back. But I realized that I needed to expand my social circle. Since moving to Tucson, most of the people I knew were teachers. Many of them are still my closest friends, but they had day jobs. I needed to find someone to share my interests and availability at this stage of my life.

My career in education had trained me well; I was an expert in looking for resources. After a brief computer search I found what I was looking for:

(Your town's Name) Social Seniors
60+ social and searching? Coffee,
companionship, friendship, camaraderie and things
to do sound interesting? Here you will find fun events
for Active, Social and Independent Seniors that will
bring you out to have new experiences, learn
something new and make new friends!

Five upcoming events were listed: four morning coffee talks, and for the more adventurous, one afternoon happy hour. In order to join, the organizers required an online profile including a recent photo. The rules stated that if you had three "no-shows" you would be removed from the group. I wondered who would be taking attendance. Probably a retired teacher.

I considered it, but decided to try something less structured first. My friend (and former teammate) Lisa recommended a neighborhood women's gym she attended after school and on weekends. She knew that many *others* visited during the day. (She started to say *older people,* but quickly corrected herself.) I decided to give it a try. It would be a chance to meet people, and I could work on whittling away the waistline rolls I'd accumulated during my hibernation period.

On my first day, the owner greeted me and showed me how to use the equipment. Peppy, upbeat music filled the room, and the clients rotated around the circle of exercise equipment to complete their workout. At the signal everyone moved one spot to the left. *Ha!* I thought to myself, *This is just like the rotating stations I'd set up in my kindergarten classroom.*

At first I concentrated on working the equipment and making sure I was moving at the sound of the "change stations now" command. I was huffing and puffing so much that it was impossible to carry on a conversation. I'm not a gym person, but it was nice to be in a women-only space. No one worried about cellulite popping out of spandex or underarm "batwings" flapping.

I got to know some of the nine o'clock ladies as we moved through the exercise circuit together. Celia didn't need to worry about jiggly parts. She was toned, fit and fierce, blazing through the circuit. Lucille, in her capris, matching tee shirt and beauty-shop hair, barely moved the weights. A cancer survivor, brave Gwen arrived on the city bus and moved slowly as she regained her strength.

One morning the gym was quiet. Although the invigorating music was playing, we plodded through our workout on autopilot. Since no one was talking, I focused on the music. The exaggerated disco beat had distorted the melody, but the words were clear. A smile spread across my face as I recognized the Rolling Stones tune.

"Hey ladies!" I said, "They are playing our song!"

There was no response.

47

"You know...*Honky Tonk Women!*" I sang out the refrain as it blasted from the speakers. The musical reference to dancing saloon girls (or prostitutes) cracked me up as I looked around at my fellow silver-haired, spandex-clad workout buddies.

That got their attention. Some sang along, a few looked at me as if I were crazy, but our overall tempo picked up, and we finished strong. We laughed and chatted through the rest of the routine and even broke out the hula hoops to celebrate the end of the workout.

Sadly, the gym went out of business before I could establish any lasting friendships, but it was a start. Like a shy child on the first day of kindergarten I had been timid at first, yet I found I still knew how to make friends. With my confidence boosted, I didn't need that senior meet-up site yet, but if I ever changed my mind I knew what to put on my profile sheet:

"Retired teacher, enjoys pumping iron, the Rolling Stones, and plays well with others."

That should attract some interesting people.

The Two-Hour Cruise

Summer vacation. It's funny I was still calling it that even though every day was a vacation now. I was sitting on the porch swing overlooking Eagle Bay at our family condo in southern Indiana. Ed and I had scheduled a few weeks to return to our hometown. We hoped to escape the Arizona heat and spend time with our families. It was cooler here, the giant tulip trees shaded the porch this time of day, but the air was thick with moisture. Beads of condensation ran off the glass of iced tea and dripped onto my lap, while the muggy air made my shirt stick to my back.

My history with this place began one October day in 1999. According to family folklore, the real estate agent opened the sliding glass door and our father stepped onto the deck. He stood in silence for several moments as he gazed out on crystal blue waters fringed with the brilliant colors of Indiana's autumn. When at last he found his words, he turned to Mom and said, "You can keep looking but this is our place." At least, that's how our mother, Alice, tells the story. They purchased the property and planned to move in when Dad retired. It was to be their place, a retreat for family and friends.

Six months later, my father died. After the public funeral at church, we had a private memorial at the condo. Mom wanted us to scatter some of Dad's ashes off the porch, towards the lake view he loved. One by one, my siblings and I stepped onto the deck. I never told my mother, but I wasn't able to put my hand into the box of ash and bone that was my dad. I didn't want to scatter him. He should have been here with us, whole and strong. It would be many years before I could bring myself to return.

My siblings and I are now the caretakers of the lakeside condo and we use it as a family gathering spot. Dad would've liked that. Though he never got to enjoy it, Dad's condo was fulfilling its intended purpose.

The rhythmic creak of the porch swing kept pace with the lazy afternoon. A month had passed since my retirement luncheon in the school cafeteria and I struggled with the abruptness of my exit from teaching. I longed for closure, a rite of passage to signal my entrance to this next stage of life. My career deserved to be celebrated. I thought of my mother. What would Alice do?

"Well, for starters, I wouldn't sit around moping. I'd get off that swing and throw myself a party." The clarity of my mother's voice in my head caused me to

laugh out loud. Throw a party... that's exactly what Mom would do.

When a friend of mine retired from her position as a business manager, she took her entire family on a Caribbean cruise. They spent a week together enjoying fine dining, snorkeling, swimming, and just hanging out together. I loved this idea, but Ed and I needed to be careful with our money. The term "fixed income" crept into our conversations now. Besides, it was a little late to be pulling something like that together. Still, wouldn't it be fun to do *something*?

I was watching a sailboat on the lake when an idea came to me. My son, Matt, and his family were arriving from Atlanta in a few days and my daughter, Kelli, and her family lived nearby. We could still do a cruise! I called the local marina to see what might be available.

"Well, honey, it's pretty late notice," the Marina Lady replied in her Hoosier drawl. "We gotta party boat available for that date. You wanna party boat? They're kinda expensive but they're real nice. Double-decker with a two-story slide. It can hold up to thirty people and we can hook up a keg for ya."

I wanted a party, and I pictured my three grand-daughters zipping down the slide and splashing into the lake, but the huge party boat with the keg seemed excessive.

"Don't you have anything smaller?" I asked.

"Nope, sorry. Well now wait a minute... we gotta ten-seater pontoon comin' in at 5:30 that day. Let's see... it'll take us a bit to clean and refuel it. You can have it from six 'till it gets dark. You'd have to have it back by eight in the evening."

The time frame wasn't what I wanted. I had pictured us out on the lake all day, but we could work with it. I booked the ten-seater pontoon, called a sandwich shop to order cold cut sandwiches, chips, and cookies, and invited my family to go on a two-hour dinner cruise to celebrate my retirement.

The three granddaughters were ecstatic. We got the old life jackets out of the hall closet and practiced putting them on. Our adult children got into the act by downloading boat themed music for our traveling soundtrack including "The Banana Boat Song," the theme from "Gilligan's Island," and some songs from modern artists that had adult words in them. They thought this was hilarious and threatened to crank up the volume when we got to those songs. If not for their under-aged children present, I'm sure they would have followed through with their threat. Since we didn't get the boat with the keg, I put my son, Matt, and my son-in-law, Chris, in charge of getting an assortment of drinks for the cooler.

We loaded the car and started out on an overcast southern Indiana evening. As Ed went into the marina office to sign paperwork, the grandchildren and I walked to the end of the pier to watch the boats. One of the large party boats was just returning for the evening, its end-of-the-year college celebration winding down. The passengers, dressed in cut-off shorts and bathing suits, looked as if they had made good use of the kegs and water slide.

"Wow! Is that going to be our boat?" asked Lillian eyeing the giant water slide.

"No, sorry, honey," I replied, hoping she wouldn't be disappointed.

Ed emerged from the rental office with the paperwork secured and our group made its way to the slip. We held on to each other as we stepped from the solid dock onto the wobbly deck of the boat. After making sure that the younger ones had life jackets on, Captain Ed took the first turn behind the wheel. It occurred to me that he had never driven a boat before, but how hard could it be? After a few false starts, and nearly running into the party boat, we headed out to open water and the Two-Hour Retirement Cruise was launched.

Heavy, gray clouds hung low in the sky and a light rain dabbed our faces as we navigated along the main part of the lake, but that just became part of the fun. As the weather started getting rough, Matt found the "Gilligan's Island" song on the playlist and the adults began to sing, shouting out the words over the churning of the boat's motor:

Our grandchildren thought we were crazy, but they each took a turn behind the wheel. The "fearless crew "navigated us towards Eagle Bay just as the sun began to break through the clouds. From the inlet I saw the back deck of our condo peeking out from the dense, green foliage of the trees. I had never viewed it from this angle. It was the deck which had enchanted Dad, the deck I had stood on eighteen years ago after his funeral. If my sister and brothers had been braver than I during the ash-scattering ceremony, it's possible that a little of Dad landed on this very shore. It was a new perspective for me. A lost piece of my heart slipped back into place.

The splash of the anchor hitting the water signaled it was time to stop for the fine dining part of the cruise. We passed around paper plates and distributed sandwiches, chips, and cookies. The cooler supplied an assortment of soft drinks, beer, and wine. The granddaughters sat on the back deck of the boat dangling their feet in the cool water. Shoulder to shoulder in their puffy life vests they formed a rainbow-colored stair step: twelve-year-old Michaela, nine-year-old Melanie, and seven-year-old Lillian. Giggles and screams erupted when they thought fish were nibbling at their toes.

As dinner concluded, we raised our drinks and toasted my retirement. The setting sun broke through the last remnants of the clouds streaking them with orange, pink, and gold, and the water was calm as we made our way back to the marina. I remember thinking, *so here's what you get for your many years of service... a two-hour pontoon boat ride around the local lake with your family, singing silly songs, eating sandwiches, and drinking wine from a can.* It was the perfect rite of passage. Thanks Dad, for this place of healing. And Mom, I took your advice and threw myself a party. I had earned it.

***

After our company left, I had a few more days to enjoy some quiet time at the condo on the lake. I was beginning to put closure on my career, yet there was one more thing I needed. Sitting on the porch with my morning cup of tea, I was just a few miles from where it had all begun. Maybe it was time to pay my past a visit and come to terms with the magnitude of how far I had come.

Part Two

Road Trip

"I have great respect for the past. If you don't know where you've come from, you don't know where you are going."

~ Maya Angelo

Stinesville Elementary

"This is it! Turn here!" I blurted.

There were no cars behind us on the highway, and Ed cut onto the narrow country road, sending a spray of gravel behind us. As we wound our way towards the tiny village of Stinesville in southern Indiana, we passed familiar landmarks. Weathered barns and crumbling silos marked the passage of time. When we passed the old general store and post office and headed up the steep hill, the two-story limestone school came into view. The sight took me back to the summer of 1975.

***

Recently married and fresh out of college, I prepared for my first job interview.

"You're going to need a good suit for interviews," Mom had said as I looked at my reflection in the dressing room mirror. I had done my research. The school dress code stated that while the administration preferred women teachers wear professional dress (i.e., dresses or skirts), they would allow slacks if worn with a matching jacket. The polyester jacket-and-slacks ensemble constricted me, a far cry from the slouchy, faded jeans and loose fitting tops I'd worn in college. At twenty-two years old, I hoped the trendy sage-green color and belted waistline would offset the matronly way I felt.

The gymnasium was stuffy the night of my interview, making me too warm in my new pantsuit. The slick fabric caused me to slide around on the metal folding chair as I faced the principal and school board members. My hands trembled as I placed my folder on the table and mentally ran through answers to questions I was certain they would ask. I was over-prepared.

"Do you think you can teach kindergarten? We've got a half-day opening."

"I have a kindergarten endorsement and I did student teaching in kindergarten this spring..." I began as I inched my credentials towards the principal.

"Can you start next week?"

No one asked to see my excellent grade point average, my transcripts, or my letters of recommendation. They offered me a job on the spot, half-day kindergarten at Stinesville Elementary. The contract confirmed that I would be teaching a morning session of kindergarten and my annual salary would be $3,500. I was elated.

As a last minute addition to the staff, I rushed to put up bulletin boards and decorate my room. I enlisted the help of my grandpa to make a two-sided, hinged wooden structure out of sheets of plywood to form the outline of a playhouse. When I arranged the child-sized stove, refrigerator, and doll bed inside, it was perfect. The block corner was well supplied with the standard wooden blocks and toy cars and trucks. Bookshelves from home lined the library corner and two paint easels were set up by the sink. When I saw the veteran teacher next door had curtains for her windows, I brought my sewing machine in and made some for my room, pleased with the homey touch it invoked.

And so my teaching career began. As I'd boasted in my expedited interview, I had a kindergarten endorsement and a successful student teaching experience. How hard could it be? Um... way harder than I had expected. Though eager and full of ideas, nothing in my college courses had prepared me for the challenges I faced. I learned by trial and error. Mostly error. My first day was a disaster.

It was school picture day, and it had taken me all morning to corral my thirty-one rambunctious five-year-olds and get them in line with their hair combed and Sunday-best clothes smoothed out. Teacher assistants were a thing of the future; I was on my own. Somehow I lost a kid. Apparently, one of my students didn't want to get his picture taken and ran out of the gym as we stood in line waiting for the photographer. I didn't notice the loss until the principal brought him back to my room later that morning. Her scowl let me know I wasn't off to a very good start.

Classroom management continued to be my nemesis throughout that first year. No college class taught me how to collect "milk money" and have it recorded and turned into the office by 8:15 while my class was finding more interesting things to do. There was no "How to Line-up Your Students" class offered at Ball State University. As a saving grace, my energetic pupils would sit quietly for story time, and the more animated I became, the more attentive they were. We must have read every book in the school library at least twice. To this day, I pride myself on my storytelling voice born out of desperation.

At the end of the year, when my contract was in jeopardy of being cancelled, the principal intervened on my behalf. As disastrous as that first year was, she must have seen something in me that made her convince the school board I deserved another chance. My contract was renewed and I stayed for two more years until Ed's job took us to a new city.

**

Traveling down the country road to Stinesville that summer afternoon had transported me back in time. Memories, still vivid and fresh in my mind, made it seem like yesterday, yet it had been over four decades since I'd taught in that building. They'd locked the doors to the old limestone structure, and a sign indicated the space was now a community center. I snapped a few photos of the building and smiled to myself. I had something in common with that old girl.

Having dedicated our lives to education, we were both being repurposed. As I got back in the car, it occurred to me that it might be fun to visit all of my schools, take a picture or two, and jot down some memories. In the first summer of retirement, my quest began. Over the next few weeks, I journeyed through southern Indiana to retrace my professional path.

Nashville Elementary

Nashville, Indiana is a sleepy little town nestled in the hills of Brown County in the southern part of the state. Its residents are an interesting mix of rural folks and artists. Tourists flock to visit the area in the fall when abundant deciduous trees explode in brilliant color across the landscape. You can still get fried biscuits and homemade apple butter at the local general store and cafe. Small farms dot the rolling hills and change comes slowly. Public school kindergarten was a new concept in 1978. Nashville Elementary had never had a kindergarten program, and it was obvious the principal was nervous.

"I'm *pretty* sure it will be alright," he fretted as he showed me around. I imagined he had visions of unruly five-year-olds running amuck in his building.

They'd stocked the room with some basics: wooden building blocks, small tables and chairs, and a child-sized stove and refrigerator for the housekeeping area. Grandpa's playhouse structure would fit right in. An ancient upright piano stood in the corner. They had assumed the newly hired kindergarten teacher could play. I would rely on my

63

record collection and guitar, but the old piano added a quaint touch to the space. It would make a novel room divider topped off with some potted plants. My fish aquarium would fit in one corner of the room. I'd have to scour the school library for books to fill the shelves, but yes, I could make this place work for my two half-day kinder-garten sessions. By now, I had three years of teaching experience behind me and I approached the year with confidence.

"The room is perfect," I reassured the principal. "It's going to be a great year!"

And it was. With no state standards or teacher manuals for kindergarten, I was free to follow my heart. We learned the alphabet and numbers by singing songs, building with blocks, taking turns in the housekeeping corner, caring for our pet fish, planting seeds and watching them grow—all the things that made me fall in love with early childhood education. With limited funds available for art supplies, I perfected my playdough recipe at home by cooking the sticky flour, water, and salt mixture until it reached the proper consistency. A local philanthropic organization donated money for craft paper, paint, and paste. I still remember the smell as I scooped out gooey globs of the sticky stuff from a gallon jar and put it into recycled butter tubs, one for each table, hoping my supply would last through an entire year of crafts.

"Don't eat the paste, it will make you sick!" I'd reminded my students more than once. "Besides, we need it for our art projects."

A blizzard hit right before Christmas break that year. Several feet of snow blanketed the hills, county roads were impassable, and schools were closed indefinitely. No one worried about it. We didn't make up any of the days, and to the best of my knowledge, no one was permanently scarred for having missed a few weeks of school. When we resumed classes in mid-January, we threw out the dried up Christmas tree and picked up where we left off. As a bonus, the paste supply held out until we fastened construction paper flowers to the Mother's Day cards that May and sticky hands carried them home to their moms with pride.

I think I could have spent my entire teaching career in this little country school but life had other plans. Our adoption papers had been accepted, and Ed and I were moving up on the agency's list. With high expectations, I resigned my position from Nashville Elementary and made preparations to become a mom.

Clifty Creek Elementary

After leaving Nashville, we moved to Columbus, Indiana, and I put my career on hold. I took the next ten years "off" to...let's see...begin a family (we had two children now), buy a house, get a dog, and, oh yes, complete my master's degree.

Kelli was beginning kindergarten, and Matt was nearly two when I considered returning to the classroom. I loved being a full-time mom and cherished the time I'd had with my babies, yet a part of me missed my career. Finances also entered into my decision. We'd managed as a one-income family, but funds were tight. After weighing my options, I took a chance, got my resume together, and submitted it to the Bartholomew Consolidated School Corporation in the fall of 1985. My friend prepared me for disappointment.

"You won't get in; it's competitive. I know someone who's tried for years. She even worked as a substitute teacher in the district, and she's still waiting for a job offer."

I knew she was right; my resume would be one of hundreds. If I had any chance of getting a job, I'd have to be assertive, something that went against my nature. Two weeks before the start of school, I visited each principal in person to introduce myself and hand him or her my resume. It was a risky move; quite likely I would get a few doors slammed in my face, but I persevered. My gamble paid off. By the end of the week, two principals had offered me kindergarten positions. My kindergarten endorsement and experience were in great demand, and both schools needed to fill last minute needs due to unexpected enrollment.

The new construction of Clifty Creek Elementary won me over with its award-winning architecture and bright open kindergarten wing, complete with its own kitchenette. After my experience in rural schools, I felt like I had moved up to the big league. My salary of $18,500 reinforced that feeling. I found a neighbor who was starting a daycare for teacher's kids, and she welcomed Matt into her small group. She was also willing to look after Kelli before and after kindergarten. Soaring into fall, I congratulated myself on how well things were working out.

My confidence was short lived. Now the mother of a toddler and a five-year-old, my mornings were hectic and there was little time to relax in the evenings. Besides, kindergarten expectations were higher than they had been when I'd taught in Nashville ten years ago. We had a detailed kindergarten report card and a state curriculum to follow. I struggled to keep up my expectation of being a perfect mom and teacher, convincing myself I could do it all. The crash came at Thanksgiving.

We'd spent weeks preparing for our kindergarten feast. A teepee made of bean poles (donated from a local farm family) and sheets stood in the corner. We sat in a circle and passed a jar of whipping cream around, each child shaking it until a lump of pale butter formed. This would accompany the Jiffy-mix cornbread we'd baked the day before. The room was full of parent volunteers, eager to share this experience with their kindergartener. I stationed some at the cooking table where they opened cans or helped students chop fresh fruit for the Friendship Fruit Salad. Others helped students thread macaroni beads onto lengths of yarn to form necklaces.

When all was ready, the parents helped the students put on the Native American vests we'd made of paper sacks or construction paper Pilgrim hats and collars. We pushed the classroom tables together to make one long "Thanksgiving style" table, set with student-made placemats, plastic forks, and paper plates. After a word of thanks, the feast began. It was a lovely sight. The kids were having a good time, and the parents seemed impressed.

If I could have frozen that moment, I would have retired right then, bathed in the golden glow of teaching magic. But real life soon interrupted my bliss. Within five minutes, the pilgrims and Native

Americans had turned into turkeys. They gobbled down their food, or picked at it, and looked for something more interesting to do—such as chase each other around the room. I panicked as I glanced at the clock and realized it would be an hour and a half until dismissal time and I had nothing else planned. Too late, I'd learned three of the hard and fast rules of teaching: timing is everything, plan way more than you think you will need, and expect the unexpected.

Somehow I pulled it together. The volunteers cleaned up the remnants of the feast while I entertained the troops. When they tired of songs and games, I resorted to the Hail Mary of teaching and took the class out for an extra-long recess. The minutes crept towards the dismissal time. After waving goodbye to the last of the carpool line, I collapsed into my chair. I had fifty minutes to regroup before repeating the entire scene when the afternoon class arrived. I couldn't face it.

On wobbly knees, I headed to the counselor's office and asked to use her phone to call my husband. Seeing the look on my face, she asked no questions and shut the door behind her as she left. I lost it.

"It was a mistake to go back to teaching," I sobbed into the phone. I can't do this job... it's... too... hard." The details of my disastrous morning came pouring out.

"Ok, ok. Calm down," Ed said. Then he delivered one of the greatest half-time talks of all time. "Pull yourself together. You know what went wrong this morning. Work on your timing. You can do this; you're an excellent teacher. Now, eat your lunch and get back in there. We can talk when you get home."

The second Thanksgiving feast went much better. I knew where I'd gone wrong and made adjustments. We took our time getting ready for the feast and I had a Thanksgiving themed bingo game ready to play as the students finished eating. When we talked that night, Ed asked if I thought I could make it through the first semester. We agreed if I wanted to resign after Christmas break, we could work together to make it happen.

There are moments in my career I can pinpoint as being significant. This was one. I stood on the edge of a major decision. Teaching wasn't always golden-glow moments. It was going to be arduous work, especially with the added responsibilities of motherhood. I would need grit—that combination of courage, conscientiousness, perseverance, resilience, and passion—to carry me through. Something deep inside pushed me forward.

I made it through the first semester, and Clifty Creek Elementary became my professional home for the next 16 years. It's where our children, Kelli and Matt, spent their elementary-school days growing and learning in classrooms just down the hall from my kindergarten, or later, first grade room. This environment was an excellent training ground for me.

The district encouraged new ideas, and teachers experimented with the curriculum. "Shelve the textbooks and use real-world applications" was the philosophy of the time. I taught reading using the Four Block Method, hands-on math with "Box It Bag It" math materials, and spent hours writing and implementing yearlong thematic instruction. I developed a passion for learning alternative ways to teach and sought novel experiences for my students.

It is here that I learned two important things about myself as a teacher. One, this was a career that would be constantly changing and that for me, being a "learner" was just as exciting as being a "teacher." Secondly, this profession was never going to be easy. In order to survive I would need to surround myself with the most talented people I could find, and I learned the joys of team teaching and collaboration. And grit? I was soon going to need it more than ever.

Fodrea Community School

If Columbus, Indiana, had been large enough, its "inner city school" would have been Fodrea. Built in the early 70s, and following the educational philosophy of the time, the architect designed it as an open-concept building. Large open spaces allowed for group activities and team teaching. In order to build kid-friendly and playful spaces, the building included two interior slides students could use to get from one level to the next. Ultimately, the open concept trend in education fell out of favor, and by the time I arrived in 2001 the space had undergone many renovations to include classroom walls and more traditional spaces. Due to budget constraints, the slides remained, though walled off at the top to prevent students from using them. Apparently the architect's vision of fun had been a major source of accidents and discipline issues. Imagine that.

I made the move to Fodrea because I was interested in their balanced calendar. Originally designed to accommodate working parents, the schedule was arranged in four nine-week blocks with a three week intersession in between each one, thus eliminating the long summer break. Students had the option to attend inter sessions to receive remedial and enrichment opportunities. The kindergarten space remained open-concept, meaning there were no walls separating the two kindergarten classrooms. Some years we had up to sixty students working with two teachers and four teacher assistants. I worked with my teaching team to perfect student learning stations. Students would move through the day rotating through six adult-led stations, each designed to reinforce basic skills with developmentally appropriate activities. I learned "one size does not fit all" and I had to constantly modify the curriculum to meet diverse student needs.

Fodrea was a Title I school with a high percentage of students living at or below the poverty level. I knew it was going to be tough, but nothing in my personal life or teaching experience prepared me for the challenges my students faced. There was a comaradery among the staff unlike any I have ever experienced. It's almost like we were in a war zone. We held each other up and depended on each other, believing, *knowing*, we made a difference in the lives of our students. This kept us going through the daily challenges. The years I spent in this community school were some of the most rewarding of my career. But make no mistake, the work was exhausting, often pushing us to the breaking point. I almost ended my career here after the thwarted chair-throwing episode, but ultimately challenged myself to persevere.

By the end of my nine-year tenure at Fodrea, the winds of educational change were blowing once again, and contemporary educational philosophies demanded a new physical layout. Over the summer, they would transform the school into one of the district's Signature Academies, a showcase for project-based-learning instruction.

As the last group of students left for the summer, the demolition crews moved in, marking the walls that were going to come down. They painted a large X on the side of the slide that had once invited students to zoom down into the kindergarten room. One of the last remnants of the original 1970s building, it deserved to have a ceremony. A group of us gathered at the top of the old slide.

My teacher assistant cried, "Let's do it!"

One by one, my colleagues stepped over the restraining wall and slid on their butts, laughing and shouting as those first few students must have done. When my turn came, I paused for just a moment at the top. It was a steep drop, straight down, with no up-turn at the end. I remembered the old stories about students who'd broken bones on this very slope and almost talked myself out of it.

Oh, what the heck. It's a fitting tribute to the old building that had been home to so many. Besides, I've always wanted to do this, I told myself as I pushed off. The ride was swift and my backside hit the ground hard. With a jolt, I ushered in the next stop on my professional journey.

Columbus Signature Academy

The metamorphosis of Fodrea Community School to Columbus Signature Academy, Fodrea Campus (or CSA Fodrea) was dramatic. The new layout included bright learning spaces and state-of-the-art technology. One of three campuses in Columbus designated as a project-based-learning school, we taught basic skills and state standards within the context of student-led inquiries and projects. It was a fresh approach to learning with a staff that shared a common focus.

The kindergarten rooms shared an open wall to allow for team teaching and student collaboration between the two classes. Each classroom contained a large smart board. Classroom tables were mobile so I could arrange the room as needed for the project at hand. Educators were no longer referred to as "teachers." The orange and white name tag I wore read:

Mrs. Van Deventer
Kindergarten Facilitator

It was a far cry from my humble beginnings at Stinesville Elementary. By this time, expectations for teachers and students were high and accountability was the new buzzword. We checked our kindergarten students against rigorous state and national standards and expected them to exit the year knowing how to read, do basic addition and subtraction problems, and write a multi-sentence story. Administrators assessed educators using a four-page rubric and assigned a score that had implications for compensation. In addition, the state used student assessment data to influence funding. The stakes were high.

Kindergarten was now a full-day program. Finding it difficult to fit everything in, my co-teacher and I strived to make every minute count. Teamwork and a commitment to our weekly joint planning sessions was crucial in making it all work. The challenge, as I saw it, was to maintain a sense of fun for my young students, and myself, while tackling a challenging curriculum. Make the work seem like play. Because CSA Fodrea was a showcase school for educators across the state, we frequently had visitors. On a typical morning a guest might experience:

The lively chatter of five-year-olds rings through the room. A small group of wiggly students face the digital smart board as I lead them through the morning's phonics lesson.

"b...u...s," I make the sound of each letter as I move my hand from left to right across the screen.

*"Now let's blend these sounds together... bus!"
The students sound out the word with me. As I tap
the smart board, an animated school bus moves
across the chalkboard-sized screen.*

*Across the room, a teacher assistant is leading
another group of children in an alphabet fishing
game.*

*"I caught one! I caught one!" a student cries out
as he admires the paper fish that is dangling by a clip
on the end of the magnet-hook fishing pole.*

*"Good job, Ryan! What letter is on it?" the
teacher assistant asks.*

"D!" he shouts in triumph.

*In one corner of the room, we arranged child-
sized kitchen furniture to resemble a restaurant. One
student sits at the tiny table and reads the menu
while one of her classmates writes her order. Two
other students take plastic food out of the petite
refrigerator and cook it on the play stove.*

*An argument breaks out over whose turn it is to
be the customer. The cook is about to hit the
customer on the head with a plastic skillet. Students
at the nearby playdough station glance up from their
letter stamping activity in alarm as the situation in
the restaurant escalates. The teacher assistant leaves
the fishing game and moves in to restore order.*

*Just then, the smart board timer chimes. An
animated monkey swings across the screen holding a
sign that reads "Clean up time." Reluctantly, the*

students stop what they are doing and the noise level rises as they put materials back in place. It's their least favorite part of the morning. I follow a track of blue footprints and help a student remove a wad of playdough from the bottom of his shoe.

The smart board graphic changes again, and the cartoon monkey announces that it's time to move to the next station. Students look at their color-coded name tags to see which station they will go to next. A flurry of movement occurs as they search for the large colored signs around the room that match the color on their lanyard. They move to their next station and settle in. The group of students at the reading center needs my help to reset their child-sized laptops to this week's assigned story.

We repeat the process until all five groups have rotated through each station. Tomorrow, my class will go to my teaching partner's room where they will experience math-related stations while I lead her class through our language arts activities.

I'd come far as a teacher since the day the Pilgrims and Native Americans of Clifty Creek Elementary ran amuck and I had nothing planned. My hard work and experience had paid off. My students were making significant progress in large part because I understood the curriculum demands and committed myself to my goal of making our days together meaningful and fun. Yet, in my quest for perfection, had I turned into an over-scheduled clock-watcher? It's possible that the need to have every minute planned would make for a difficult transition to retirement down the road. To be honest, thoughts of retirement had crossed my mind. My children were grown, and I now had grandchildren. Ed and I were considering the possibilities of our lives after teaching when a new opportunity came my way.

Teacher Coaching
CSA Fodrea and Rockcreek Elementary

I paced the hallway as I waited for my interview. It was 2012, and it had been many years since I'd been on this side of the process. When the position of Instructional Consultant opened up in my school district, a friend encouraged me to apply.

"With your classroom experience, you'd be perfect for the job," she'd said.

I must admit, the idea intrigued me. It's not that I was unhappy with my role at CSA Fodrea. In the two years I'd been there, my teaching partner and I had worked hard to build a kindergarten program we were proud of. Yet, the opportunity to support teachers appealed to me. Eager for a change, I submitted my application.

I hadn't been waiting long when the door to the interview room popped open and a pert young teacher emerged. My heart sank. She was probably full of new ideas and a technology whiz. How could a sixty-year-old teacher who'd been in the classroom for thirty-one years compete with that? I glared at the back of my

81

competitor as she tucked her portfolio under her arm and clicked down the hallway in her stylish shoes. The principal poked her head out as I was turning back towards the door.

"We'll be right with you," she chirped, most likely influenced by the perky interviewee she'd just encountered.

The intermission gave me time to compose myself. I needed a pep talk.

Alright Deb, get a grip. Thirty years of teaching experience is exactly what they need. You know what teachers face day to day; you've been there. Besides, you've worked with many of these teachers and staff members for years. No sweet young thing right out of college can beat that. Now go in there and blow them away!

With that I hummed a refrain from a Jim Croce song that had been running through my head all morning: *moving ahead so life won't pass me by.* I squared my shoulders and held my head high. When my turn came, I strode into the room with confidence. Looking back, I wondered if I was still humming. In any case, it worked. The instructional consultation position was mine.

I began my new job the following fall. I would work with my current staff at CSA Fodrea and the teachers at Rockcreek Elementary, just a short distance away. On my first day on the job, I arrived at my office early. *My office.* I had an office! I arranged my bookshelf with reference books, added a few pictures, switched on my computer and stared at the blank screen. Now what was I supposed to do? Normally I'd be running around making sure I was ready for students to arrive. With no such agenda, I busied myself answering emails until I saw the busses pull up. Trying to make myself useful, I greeted students and helped them find their way to their new classrooms.

"*Well,* don't *you* look relaxed and rested? It must be nice," quipped a colleague as she dashed to her classroom just steps ahead of her herd of third graders.

I forgave her catty remark. If our places had been reversed, I would've thought the same thing. I spent the first few days introducing myself to the teachers and administrators I'd be working with. At the beginning-of-the-year staff meetings, I let them know I'd be available as a resource to help them come up with strategies for learning or behavioral issues. My words expressed confidence, but deep down, I was nervous. I had classroom experience and some basic training in how the consultation process worked, but would I *really* be able to help? Would teachers accept me in this new role?

On the third day of school, I met Joshua. He'd been running around the kindergarten room, refusing to follow directions and tearing up his papers. This type of behavior had been going on for several days.

On this particular day, he'd decided he'd had enough of school and positioned himself on the floor of the kindergarten bathroom. The teacher had tried everything she could think of, but Joshua refused to budge. Having run out of options, the teacher notified the principal.

"Are you ready for your first case?" she said as she stepped into my office.

And so my new role began. While sitting with Joshua on the bathroom floor, I discovered he liked monster trucks and wrestlers. After a while, I coaxed him out with a book about trucks, and he finished out the afternoon in the classroom. I breathed a sigh of relief, yet I knew it was a temporary solution. When I got back to my office, I called my mentor. Terry was the one who'd encouraged me to apply for the job, and she had several years of experience in this role.

"Oh man," she said. "Behavior cases are the hardest. You won't even get the official training for this until later in the year. You're jumping in head first with this one."

Terry directed me to the "behavior" section in my training manual and led me through the process step by step. It seemed overwhelming, but I had to help Joshua and his teacher.

It was a new focus for me. Instead of leading a class, I found myself in the role of observer, consultant, and keeper of data to evaluate the success or failure of the strategies implemented. It was a new process for teachers as well. Most appreciated the opportunity to have a partner in the classroom who could make objective observations and help them come up with strategies. Some were expecting me to wave a magic wand and resolve the issue instantaneously. In most cases, there would be no quick fix. It would take a teacher/consultant partnership and hard work in order to succeed.

Joshua's case involved lots of observations to determine the cause of his behavior and learning issues. We implemented many strategies over the next few months with minimal success. Eventually, our data showed Joshua would need specialized help. The team referred him to a special education program to meet his complex emotional and educational needs. By the end of the year, he was able to return to his kindergarten class on a part-time basis.

Besides behavior cases, I worked with teachers to implement learning centers and find strategies to help students struggling with reading and math concepts. It was the first time in my career I'd worked with students older than first grade age and I found, to my surprise, that I enjoyed their independence and the unique challenges they presented.

Along with on-the-job training, the school system provided many learning opportunities. In meetings with other consultants around the state, I took part in some of the best training I'd received in my career. I often wished I had the advantages of this training years ago. It was exciting to learn research-based strategies for learning sight words and math facts and ways to help students retain what they'd read. As schools in Columbus moved to implement district-wide initiatives, the role of Instructional Consultant evolved. Teachers sought help to navigate the complex teacher evaluation system and learning initiatives. Some thought it was a waste of time and money to pull educators out of the classroom for this purpose. I saw it as a chance to use my combined years of experience to support teachers in their ever-more-challenging role of meeting the needs of all students.

This new chapter in my professional life lasted three years. I thought it was a fitting way to wrap up my thirty-four-year career. My numbers added up, and I was eligible to retire. Additionally, the district offered an economic incentive to do so. In the spring of 2015 I celebrated my tenure with Bartholomew Consolidated School. Ed and I left Indiana and moved to Arizona. My first official retirement lasted less than three months.

Manzanita Elementary

News flash: Phoenix, Arizona, April 26, 2018: *Tens of thousands of Red for Ed supporters descended on the Arizona capitol Thursday in a historic demonstration protesting years of education budget cuts. The red-clad marchers asked for higher teacher pay and increased classroom funding for Arizona students. Arizona teacher salaries and funding per student rank near the bottom in the nation. Teachers across the state vowed to continue the protests until state legislators take steps to avert an educational crisis.*

***

A mixture of excitement and apprehension washed over me as I mounted the steps of the chartered bus on the morning of April 26. My red tee-shirt blended in with the dozens of other Tucson teachers heading for Phoenix. I glanced down at the bag a parent and her school-aged son handed me as we gathered in the high school parking lot. The student should have been in school, but there would be no classes in Tucson, or anywhere else in Arizona this day. Or the next day. Or the following week. Schools across the state had shut down, anticipating a

87

massive teacher migration during this period of protest. The brown paper sack contained red-iced sugar cookies with the words "RED for ED" written in white frosting, and a bottle of water. This, a token of encouragement and community support for the journey ahead.

Over my shoulder, I saw the building that had welcomed me during "new" teacher orientation in August 2015, ushering in my encore career as a fourth-grade teacher at Manzanita Elementary. There were butterflies in my stomach that day, too. What was I thinking? When we moved to Arizona, I'd planned to retire. Yet something inside me knew it wasn't time. My work wasn't finished. I signed on for three more years of teaching in a new state and grade level. It turned out to be the right move. I'd made new friends and learned how fourth graders, while challenging at times, were lots of fun. On the cusp of adolescence, my students could dig deep into topics such as natural disasters, the American Revolution, and Arizona history. Those of us on the bus heading to Phoenix would add our own chapter to the state's history books.

"Hey Deb, sit by me!" Kate called from her spot near the center of the bus. I'd gotten to know this first grade teacher over the past few years. Like me, she had retired from teaching in another state and was approaching her second retirement.

"Thanks. It looks like we're going to have a full bus," I commented as I settled into the seat beside her.

I wondered why I'd chosen to get on the bus that morning. Two months before, I'd announced my intention to retire. My teaching career was ending. I was on the downhill slide to the finish line, ready to coast over it. There was nothing for me to gain from taking part in this movement. And yet, I thought about the talented student teacher at our school last semester. Upon completing her degree, she'd accepted a position in another state because she couldn't pay back her student loans with the beginning teacher salary offered in Arizona. I thought about my bright, energetic teaching partner, just beginning her career, who was already looking into changing professions. I thought about the thousands of students in overcrowded classrooms or being taught by full-time substitute teachers. High levels of stress and low salaries made it difficult for our state to attract and retain teachers.

Kate and I chatted as we made our way up Interstate 10, catching up on school issues and family news as if we were going out for an afternoon of lunch and shopping. We weren't. As we approached our destination, the magnitude of our task sank in. Traffic slowed to a crawl as cars and busses jammed the streets. Honking, cheers, and signs of support erupted from the parade of vehicles decorated in crimson and white. Interspersed among the supporters were a few showing their opposition to the movement.

A man leaned out of his car window and screamed, "Get out of my way and go back to school where you belong!"

Anxious about what I might face, my body tensed.

The bus found a spot to drop us off, and we received instructions on when and where to meet that afternoon. Upon stepping off the bus, a red wave engulfed me. Teachers had fashioned red shirts, red signs, and entire red outfits. More than one red tutu was spotted in the crowd. The eerie sound of low-flying helicopters filled the air as we made national news. The explosion of color, sights, and sounds jolted my senses and should have terrified me. Instead, I was calm. This was not a hot-head red. This red crowd was passionate, to be sure, but under control. In a bizarre way, it resembled an enormous family reunion. Teachers had set up tents and shade canopies on the lawn of the capitol building to provide respite from the blazing Arizona sun. Groups shared lunches and bottles of water. A man paused to pick up the remains of someone's lunch that had missed the trash can. An improvised song sprang up.

Oh, when the teachers go walking out,
When the teachers go walking out.
Oh, I want to be in that number,
When the teachers go walking out.

I joined a few colleagues, and we snaked our way through the congested crowd. Eventually finding a spot under a canopy, we squeezed in. We pooled our resources and had lunch: peanut butter crackers, the Red-for Ed cookies, and bottles of water. For most of the day we joined the "tens of thousands" in what could be best described as a massive sit-in.

Late in the afternoon, a group of people organized a march. One lone drummer sounded a cadence, a solemn reminder of why we had come. As we marched around the State House, someone handed me a red whirligig. Held high, its fanciful petals spun on a slender breeze and buoyed my spirits. Others marchers had more specific messages, raising hand-lettered signs:

The Governor Needs a Time Out!
I'm Marching for my Future Class
(U of A student, class of 2019)
I'm a Teacher...I Can't Afford Poster Board
(written on a cardboard box)
Imagine...

And my all-time favorite paraphrased from Dr. Seuss:
Unless Someone Like You Cares a whole awful lot,
Nothing's going to get better...it's not.

We marched around the building for an hour or so. No one in the stone tower peeked out of the darkened windows or offered a word of acknowledgment. Finally, it was time for our group of Tucson teachers to go. Somehow we managed to find our bus with everyone present and accounted for, and started back. Exhausted, hot, and hungry, we flopped into our seats. The ride home was quiet as we dozed or were lost in thought.

Many teachers and supporters remained steadfast at the state capitol and were joined by others the next day. For five straight days, a sea of red gathered each morning, sending a powerful message that became impossible to ignore. Without teachers in the classrooms, education in Arizona came grinding to a halt. We didn't expect the education crisis in Arizona to improve overnight, but because of our actions, legislators took steps in the right direction. Teachers across the state returned to classrooms, convinced they'd impacted the future of education in Arizona.

So why did this soon-to-be-retired teacher get involved? I guess I was one of the "someones" who cares a whole awful lot about students, teachers, and the future of public education. I didn't coast to the finish line after all. The thirty-seven-year race was over, and I finished strong. My work was done, my swan song complete. I was prepared to hand off the baton to the next generation of educators and retire. This time it felt right.

***

Thirty-seven years. From my shaky start at Stinesville to marching for teacher's rights, I'd given it my all and was proud of the work I had done. A lifetime, really. But, then again, not an entire lifetime. I was about to learn that my life didn't end with retirement, it would simply change. With my teaching career behind me, I had time to think about what I wanted to do next. I had a feeling there would be much more to come.

Part Three

Renaissance

"Travel far enough, you meet yourself."
~ David Mitchell

Go See the World

Having survived my first summer of retirement, I was settling into my new morning routine. The sound of the school bus going through the neighborhood no longer panicked me. I was still in my pajamas enjoying a cup of tea and the morning paper when my phone rang. The conversation with my mother started off the same as always.

"Are you working?"

"No, Mom, I retired this spring."

"Oh. Is Ed working?"

"No, he's retired too."

"That's right. I knew that." She paused.

This is where my mother usually asked what we were doing with our free time, implying that we should keep busy. Instead she said, "You two have been working for so many years. Go see the world." Maybe it was the Alzheimer's talking, or perhaps Mom was having a moment of clarity. Sometimes it's hard to tell the difference, but, either way, this sounded like wonderful advice to me. I had been a traveler once... long ago.

1973

As a college student at Ball State University in Muncie, Indiana, I had the opportunity to take classes at the college's London Center in England. I'd never been out of the country before and now I was living far away from my Midwestern home. My world suddenly expanded.

Students taking part in the London Center stayed at the Glen Hotel, a bed-and-breakfast establishment that the college had converted into a makeshift dorm and classroom space. When I arrived in early spring, the weather was damp and cold. I didn't mind, I was in London! Each morning I headed downstairs to the cozy dining room. Here I was greeted by classmates and a complete English breakfast of cereal, sausage, eggs, toast and pots of strong Earl Grey tea. Everyone figured out that it was best not to miss this because it was one of the two meals provided at the Glen with our meal vouchers. The lunch menu consisted of a tub of peanut butter, a jar of strawberry jam, and a loaf of bread set out in the hallway on a TV tray. Our dinner tickets allowed us to venture out to the Gypsy Pot, a mom and pop restaurant, where we had a choice of several entrees. The beige glob of Chicken a la King served with a side of fries wasn't appealing, but it was filling and cheap. Sometimes, if we had a little extra cash, we splurged and went to a local pub for supper, taking advantage of the lower drinking age.

Everyone took the same elective courses in art appreciation, music appreciation, and history. Some of the classes met in the hotel dining room after they had cleared away the morning breakfast. Often our British professors would take us to the very places where art lived. We visited masterpieces at the Tate Gallery and the British Museum, saw Shakespeare plays and operas at the Royal Albert Hall, and spent days wandering through the displays at the Museum of Natural History.

On weekends we would head out to tour the countryside. Since none of us had a car and we were living on student budgets, we would get a group of two or three together, take public transportation to a major highway, hold up our signs showing where we wanted to go, and hitchhike. It occurs to me that we should've been concerned about our safety, but we weren't. We were young and carefree, and it was a common way to explore England. Girls felt more secure if a guy went along and the guys found that they got picked up quicker if they had a female companion. We spent the nights in youth hostels and pooled our resources to buy food at the local markets.

This type of travel isn't without risks, however. One weekend I returned from a trip to the Lake District with my right hand bandaged.

"What happened to you?" my roommate asked.

"I broke my finger," I replied.

"Oh my gosh! How did you do that?"

98

"Hitchhiking. I was holding up our sign and had my thumb sticking out. A van came around the corner and hit my hand before I stepped back. I'm OK though. The next morning we found a clinic, and they bandaged my broken finger to the one next to it. I'll be fine."

My splinted finger made doing homework difficult for a few weeks, but it was a modest price to pay for adventure. Skiers break legs. Hitchhikers break thumbs, or in my case, fingers. It makes for a rebellious story: my one and only claim to being a "wild child." Unless you count the fact that I've always wanted to be a singer in a rock-and-roll band. I can do a Janis Joplin impersonation that raises eyebrows.

The trip influenced my life in another way. Ed and I had known each other since high school. When we ended up going to the same college, we spent more time together. We found that we had a lot in common and we enjoyed each other's company. When the London Center opportunity came along, we had become close friends. Ed was eager and signed up to leave with the inaugural group, scheduled during the fall of 1972. I waited until the following spring.

The time Ed and I spent away from each other proved to be the catalyst for a budding romance. We missed each other and sent letters describing life at the London Center or back at the Muncie, Indiana campus. I remember sitting under a tree in Hyde Park one beautiful spring day rereading a letter from Ed. "I love you," he said. When I returned from England that summer we moved our status from "friends" to "dating," though it has been a long-standing joke in our fifty-year relationship that he's never asked me out on an actual date. We were and are still best friends who fell in love. Two years later, at the start of our senior year in college, we married.

We dreamed of going back to England but never found the right moment. Like most young couples, the ebb and flow of our daily lives engulfed us. We finished college, began our careers, became parents. We navigated through the years, weathering countless challenges and cherishing celebrations. Our English vacation always seemed to get put on hold as more pressing matters commanded our time and resources. Decades slipped by.

2018

As soon as we both retired, we began to plan our trip. The travel agent suggested that September would be a marvelous month to visit England. Children would be back in school and the weather would be nice. That made sense, but I sometimes think Ed anticipated I would be restless that first year and scheduled our vacation for fall so I wouldn't be tempted to return to teaching. Smart thinking.

We convinced our friends, Scott and Ann, to accompany us for the first two weeks of the journey.

We met up in Atlanta and boarded our overnight flight to Heathrow. Our excitement level ran high as we settled into our seats. We tried to be sophisticated world travelers; we behaved— embarrassingly enough—like children.

"Oh look, movies!"

"We get to choose our meals!"

"Yes, I *would* take a glass of wine!"

"What is this heated towel for?"

"Here comes more food."

"How much longer?"

Eventually we slept a little, arriving at Heathrow early the following morning. After a wild shuttle ride, we settled into the rented apartment that would be our home for the week. We ventured out into the neighborhood for groceries, found a wonderful pizzeria, and headed back to our flat for some excellent wine and conversation. We couldn't wait to begin our adventure.

The September air was cool and crisp. The blue-gray London sky peeked through autumn trees that first morning as we merged with commuters and walked the short distance to the subway station. Ed proved to be an expert in underground navigation as we made our way to all the famous spots that first week. We toured Buckingham Palace, Trafalgar Square, the British Museum, The Churchill War Room, The Tower of London, The Globe Theatre, and Piccadilly Circus. We ended each day back at our apartment with crackers, cheese, salami, pastries, or other interesting things we picked up at the market. As we opened a bottle of wine, we would relive the day's adventure.

One evening we engaged in a lively discussion about the exhibits we'd seen at the Tate Modern Gallery. It inspired me to see creativity expressed through so many mediums. I could have spent all day there. Scott had a different opinion.

"I couldn't wait to get out of the Tate," our friend confessed. "Contemporary art doesn't compare with the masterpieces we saw at the British Museum. Those Renaissance artists had genuine talent. One display at the Tate Modern was just a bunch of boxes stacked up. I don't consider that to be art. I could have done it myself."

"But it's the artist's interpretation of individuality. Did you notice that one box was a unique color? The artist was making a social commentary," I countered.

"That's not art."

We agreed to disagree. It occurred to me that it had been fun to experience such a wide variety of design and have an actual conversation with close friends about how it spoke to us individually. We were all educators, yet our conversations hadn't revolved around school topics.

During our second week in England we rented a car and left London to explore Stonehenge, Bath, Stratford-upon-Avon, Windermere, York, and

Edinburgh, Scotland. As a college student, I'd seen much of this territory by thumbing for rides and staying in youth hostels. With my hitchhiking days behind me, I was excited to be traveling in style with secure transportation and comfy accommodations.

Ed became our designated driver by default; none of the rest of us was brave enough to try. This proved to be the most exciting part of the trip as we navigated down unfamiliar, narrow streets, while driving on the left-hand side, barely missing cars and fixtures. Tensions were running high by the time we reached Stratford-upon-Avon late one afternoon. Parked cars lined the already constricted lanes leaving little room for the two-way traffic.

"Ed, you're getting too close to those cars!" I screeched from the passenger seat, which should have been the driver's seat.

"Do you want to drive?" he snapped, glaring at me. "I'm fine."

Thump.

"What was that?" I looked behind me to see something dangling from the side of the parked car we had just passed. "You broke that guy's mirror!"

"No, I didn't. They design those to fold in like that when they get tapped."

"That was more than a tap and that mirror is broken," I argued.

Ann and Scott were no help. They huddled in the back seat of the compact car, holding their breath and covering their eyes.

We *tapped* three more mirrors during our road trip. Before returning the car we stopped at a gas station and tried to buff out the scratches with paper towels. The rental agency must have been used to having cars returned by American drivers with scraped mirrors because we got by without having to pay for any damages.

Back in London, we said goodbye to our friends. Scott and Ann were heading back to the states and Ed and I spent an additional week on our own. To our amazement, we found the "Glen Hotel" where we'd stayed as college students decades ago. I had the address from a letter I'd saved, and I brought along a picture of the building taken in 1973.

"Do you think they still turn off the wall heaters when the guests leave a room?" Ed wondered.

"I doubt it." I studied the front of the building that had been our home long ago. The "Glen Hotel" sign was no longer hanging from the portico. In its place an elegant light fixture hung above the door. Though the structure had undergone a transformation, we recognized it immediately. "Remember the tubs of peanut butter and strawberry jam Mrs. Greene left in the hallway for our lunch each day? Not what I was expecting when the London Center brochure advertised: Meals Included."

"But she made a hearty English breakfast for us each morning."

"You mean, you got up in time for that?"

"Sometimes. If I hadn't been out at the pubs too late."

"You went out at night? Not me, I was studying!" I said in mock sincerity.

"Ha! Yeah, right."

We giggled and held hands, feeling like college kids again as we wandered the city with no set agenda. I couldn't get enough of the Museum of British Art and we spent an entire day at Ed's favorite, the Natural History Museum. We picked up some souvenir snow globes to bring back to the grandchildren. One afternoon, as our trip was winding down, we found a pub with outdoor tables next to the Thames River. After ordering pints of beer and sandwiches, we watched the sightseeing boats full of tourists pass by. They were just beginning their adventure. Ours was almost over.

We spent our last day in London the way we wanted to... walking around Hyde Park reminiscing. It had rained the night before and a hint of fall was in the air. The rose gardens had passed their summer splendor, but the remaining blooms were showing off their glorious colors. I searched for the tree that I was sitting under when I'd read my love letter from Ed all those years ago. Having been naïve in thinking I would remember that exact spot, I finally chose a massive oak that looked like it had been there for centuries. I sat in the damp earth under its branches long enough to snap a picture. It made a marvelous addition to our photo album, a sweet story for the grandkids. Our twenty-five-day adventure was amazing. We fell in love with each other and with England all over again.

The trip was the beginning of a personal renaissance. Being back in England brought up memories of people, places, and experiences that I hadn't thought about for years. The air was rich with art, history, literature, and culture. I breathed it in, exhilarated by possibilities.

Up in the Air

A Traveler's Tale in Four Parts

Flight Attendant

Now that I'm retired, maybe I'll be a flight attendant. That's what I'd been thinking after our trip to England. One advantage of retirement is that you have time to travel. There are many places I want to go, but airfare is expensive, so I've been thinking I could become a flight attendant. You get free flights plus a salary and an interesting wardrobe if you like short skirts and jackets with a matching scarf. The snappy ensemble comes with a choice of sensible black pumps or boots with dark tights. The lapel pins are cute.

I've been observing flight attendants, formerly known as stewardesses, for some time now, and had even looked up the requirements for employment. The stringent height, weight, and age guidelines of the past have loosened up, although you have to fit down the narrow aisle and be able to stuff heavy carry-on bags into the overhead storage compartments. There are personal grooming standards for men and women.

The airlines don't allow flight attendants to have visible tattoos, extreme piercings, or wild hair colors. I would be OK in this area unless they count gray as a wild color.

My hairdresser says that gray hair is in vogue. Some of her young clients are dying their hair to achieve this color. It's a time-consuming and expensive process to strip the hair of its color and add in the silver tones. One perk of coming of age is that I don't have to go to all that trouble.

I've seen attendants who are, shall I say, older. After watching them do their job, I know I could do it. A strategically placed neck scarf and carefully applied make-up can work wonders, and I've been pumping iron at the local ladies gym. Plus, I have experience. Having been a kindergarten teacher for many years, I'm adept at handing out snacks and an expert in bossing people around nicely.

On one of our recent flights, my husband remarked, "I'll bet that flight attendant used to be a teacher."

"How can you tell?"

"Listen to her. She has that elementary-teacher voice."

The attendant in question was making her way down the aisle.

"Sir, I've asked you twice to turn off your computer and stow it under your seat. I need you to do that *now*," she said to the man two rows ahead of us. Her face was smiling but her voice meant business. She looked him in the eye and didn't move until he had complied. I'm sure he didn't want to sit in time out, that seat in the back of the plane by the bathroom.

On second thought, maybe I don't want to be a flight attendant. It's too much like the career I just retired from.

Dangerous Snow Globes

As a flight attendant I wouldn't need to go through the TSA security lines. I must admit, however, that I'm getting good at dressing for success in this area. My standard travel outfit consists of black elastic-waist pants, slip-on shoes, a T-shirt, and a black cardigan sweater. I waltz up to the space-age-scanning tube in record time, put my hands over my head, and stand with confidence. With all systems go, I pick up my bag, slip on my shoes and am off.

Ed hates this process and grumbles. He takes off his shoes and removes his belt. Then he empties his pockets of keys, loose change, wallet, and cell phone. Finally he takes off his clunky watch and removes his hat and jacket. If he's lucky, he gets through the scanner on the first try, but more often than not, there's a leftover coin or some other object in his pocket that causes concern. Once cleared, he shuffles along in his stockinged feet, holding up his pants and clutching his shoes, watch, and wallet. I glance back at him with a sense of superiority.

I wasn't so haughty when we were returning from our trip to England. As we printed off our boarding passes at Heathrow, I saw that I had an unusual code stamped at the bottom.

"Hey, what does SSSS mean?" I asked Ed. "It's on my boarding pass."

"I'm not sure. It's not on mine," he answered.

It would soon be apparent that quadruple S is not advantageous. While we were in line, an official-looking woman with a clipboard approached us. She asked to see our passports and boarding passes.

"Where are you headed?" she asked innocently enough.

"We are going back home... Arizona... USA..." answered Ed.

"How long have you been in England?"

"Twenty-five days," Ed responded confidently.

"What were you doing in London?"

"We were sightseeing, the usual places, Buckingham Palace, The Tate Gallery, The Tower of London, things like that."

"What day were you at the Tower of London?" This time she directed her question at me and her voice took on a serious tone.

"I...I... I don't know," I stammered. "It was during that first week. I think it was a Saturday... maybe September 15?"

"Where did you stay while you were in London?"

"We rented an apartment in Drayton Park."

"The two of you?"

"Well, no, our friends stayed with us, but they took an earlier flight out, back to the US... America." Now I was getting nervous.

After a few more questions, the clipboard lady seemed satisfied and moved to ask similar questions of others in line.

"That was intense," I griped.

"It must be part of their security," Ed tried to reassure me. "This is a busy airport."

I supposed he was right, but as I came to the first security checkpoint, the agent took an unusually long time to go over my boarding pass and passport.

"Ma'am, step over here," the agent instructed.

"But, but... my husband is going that way..." I began.

"Ma'am, step over here," he ordered.

I glanced over my shoulder and signaled to Ed that I was heading to a different line. I wasn't worried. Having taken extra care that morning to make sure all liquids in my carry-on were under the three ounce limit and in clear plastic, I placed my bag on the conveyor belt and strode through the scanner. I passed through, but my bag didn't.

"Is this your bag?" a blue-gloved woman scowled.

"Yes. Is there a problem?" I asked.

"Step over here."

Oh, not again, I thought. By now Ed was out of sight, having breezed through on the fast track for once.

The woman rummaged through my bag. *Ha!* I said to myself as she pulled out my compliant toiletries. *Nothing to hide here.* Just then, she yanked her latex fingers out of my carry-on.

"What's this?" she hissed as she pointed to three small boxes wrapped in tissue at the bottom of my bag.

"Those are snow globes. My granddaughters collect them. These have London scenes and when you shake them it snows on the London Bridge... souvenirs," I nervously blabbered.

The woman stared at the boxes as if they were kryptonite.

"Unwrap them."

"But I wrapped them in their boxes so they wouldn't break."

"Ma'am, you need to unwrap them."

I did as I was told, suddenly afraid of the authority the attendant exuded. She scanned and swabbed the snow globes before she allowed me to stuff them back in my bag. Then *I* got the snow globe treatment. I had to take off my shoes and socks and she swabbed the palms of my hands and the bottoms of my feet. They patted me down before I was released.

I straggled to the lounge area, my shoes and socks in one hand and my disheveled bag in the other. When I caught up with Ed, I told him the whole sad story. He thought it was funny. The tables had turned in a big way. Now we're even and I'm not so smug when we go through security.

SSSS stands for Secondary Security Screening Selection. I looked it up. It's usually a random selection, unless they catch you with dangerous snow globes in your carry-on. Now I'm marked for life.

The Silent Treatment

Another issue for me is that once I'm on board, I don't want to start a conversation with a random passenger knowing that there will be no escape for the next several hours. I initiate a no-talking policy. I learned this lesson years ago on a trip to Atlanta.

"Where ya headed, honey?" the lady next to me asked as she attempted to stuff her oversized, gold handbag under the seat in front of her.

"I'm going to a conference in Atlanta. After that, I'll visit my son and his family in Marietta," I began.

"Girrrlllll... I tell you, they're ALL about the glitz in Atlanta!"

Was she justifying her purse or warning me that my sensible black travel outfit would stand out, in a bad way, once we landed? We introduced ourselves.

Her name was Jackie, and she was heading home to Georgia.

"You got any grandkids?" Jackie continued.

"Three girls," I said, "Two in Indiana, and one in Atlanta."

"I'll tell you what, I don't want no grandkids until I'm about sixty. By that time I figure I'll have one foot in the grave and I won't have to be taking care of no kids."

I'd passed my sixtieth birthday, I didn't feel I had one foot in the grave, and I liked my grandkids. But I was trapped in my seat. For the next three hours Jackie rambled on.

"Honey, let me tell you about this bra shop outside of Atlanta. You ever hear of the Double D-vas? They have a show on TV about women looking for the perfect fit. Most of 'em are big-chested women, and they have been wearing the wrong size bra their whole life. These bra ladies are so good, they don't even have to measure you. They just look at your boobs, and they can tell which bra to fit you in. Girl, the right bra can change your life."

By the time our flight ended, I knew more about Jackie than I did about my sister. Including her bra size. Nowadays, I make my way to my seat and settle in with a book, answering questions with terse replies and avoiding eye contact until we've landed. It's safer that way.

Moving On

When we moved to Arizona, airline travel became a necessary part of my life as I tried to keep connected to my family and friends. Some thought we were foolish to make such a drastic move across the country.

It wasn't a hasty decision. We'd passed through Tucson on a vacation and were intrigued enough to spend two summers in a rental house there. We fell in love with the turquoise sky, the saguaro cactus, the sunshine, and the way you could see a million stars in the clear night sky. Even the scorching summer temperatures didn't scare us. During one of our summer stays we contacted a realtor and looked at houses. When we returned to Indiana, we talked about what it would be like to live in the southwest. "What if..." was a game we liked to play. I remember the night we decided.

"What if we moved to Tucson?" Ed said at dinner. "The housing market is incredible out there now."

It wasn't the first time he'd started this conversation.

"But our family needs us." I echoed the sentiments of friends and family and rattled off all the reasons we should stay rooted.

"Deb, if we wait until no one needs us we'll be the ones needing help. We've lived in the same community our entire lives. Our careers are winding down and our children are on their own. This is our chance to try something new."

I looked at him across the table. His words made sense. I was terrified of moving, leaving friends and family and the home we had lived in for the past twenty-five years. I was more afraid of staying put, playing it safe, and clinging to the past. I took a gulp of wine. Then another.

"Let's do it!"

We sold our home in Indiana and contacted our realtor in Tucson. She lined up some showings, and we purchased a home in Oro Valley during our two-week fall break from school. Things fell into place nicely. With one exception.

My mother lived in an independent living apartment in Bloomington, Indiana. I went over weekly to get groceries, take her to appointments, and help organize a week's worth of her medications into the plastic pill box. It was becoming apparent that she would soon need to move to assisted living. When I announced that Ed and I were thinking of retiring to Arizona, my siblings agreed that it would make sense to move Mom to the Chicago area where she would be closer to three of her children. This freed me up to make my move across the country. Still, I was struggling with the decision and my responsibility to my mother. I would miss her.

Shortly after we moved, I took Mom to visit our new home in Arizona. She had always loved to travel and was excited to be going on an adventure. Mom sat by the window so she could see out, and I sat beside her in the middle seat. After Mom settled in, I tried to read. The words blurred before my eyes as I blinked back tears. This move was more unsettling than I thought it would be.

I glanced out the window at the clouds below. As we flew from one side of the country to the other, I felt like a balloon floating untethered between two worlds; the home I had left in Indiana and my new life in Arizona. I longed for someone to grab the string and pull me back to earth, grounding me to one spot. Who would pull the string, and where would I land? Where did I *want* to land?

Deep in thought, I retreated into my silent mode. I looked over at Mom as she slept. I knew that she had adjusted to her new home in Chicago and was close to family members there, but I felt like I had abandoned her. And yet, Mom's the one who always encouraged me to go for it, take a chance, live life to the fullest and add in a touch of glitz. That's how she had lived her life. I would need time to sort out my feelings.

The three-and-a-half hour flight from Indianapolis to Phoenix went smoothly, and we arrived without incident. As we waited to collect our bags, I asked Mom how she liked the flight.

"Well, the flight was fine," she said, "but that woman beside me was so rude. She never said a word to me the whole time."

"Mom... that woman was me. I was the one sitting next to you."

"Oh..."

We looked at each other and burst out laughing. Throughout the rest of Mom's stay we joked about "that rude woman" on the plane and wondered where she was now.

You may encounter that rude woman on her way to visit her mother in Chicago or her grandchildren in Indiana and Georgia. Or she may be off on an overseas adventure. She's the one in black hiding behind her book. Don't sit by her if you are looking for a conversationalist.

And for the record, underneath her sensible T-shirt she may be wearing a cheetah-print, perfectly fitted bra from the Double D-vas Shop in Atlanta. There's a glitzy rhinestone charm dangling from its center. Shedding her kindergarten-teacher persona, that quiet woman is secretly hoping to set off some alarms the next time she goes through security.

Seams to Sew, Stories to Weave

The rush of excitement from our trip to England was fading fast as I settled back into the slow-paced routine at home. Yet, something was different. The immersion into a different culture and the abundance of art and history I experienced on our travels was creating a change in me. The flow of creativity I once channeled into classroom projects and lesson plans ran in fresh streams as I rekindled interests that had been lying dormant for many years. Now I had time and energy to explore these passions.

I became obsessed with sewing Christmas pillowcases. Not art gallery masterpieces I'll admit, but even Michelangelo must have started off small. I can imagine him finger painting on the walls of his childhood home and experimenting with lumps of clay in the courtyard before he moved up to the Sistine Chapel and the statue of David.

I learned to sew from my mother and honed my skills through many years of 4-H, a program designed to give young people a chance to learn by doing. Each year I signed up for the sewing course and couldn't wait to get my official workbook that described the project. The result would be an item to show at the

119

county fair. Shopping for fabric with Mom was a special event. Once we made our selections, she guided me through the basics, starting with my very first project, a simple apron. Each year the projects increased in complexity. In my last year of 4-H, I made a dress for my junior prom. I fashioned the A-line, sleeveless gown from blue dotted-Swiss fabric with eyelet edging around the neck. A blue grosgrain ribbon accented the empire waist. The garment would be modest by today's prom standards, but à propos for the 1970s. I kept the dress longer than the boyfriend.

When I graduated from college, my in-laws gifted me with a state-of-the-art Sears Kenmore sewing machine. I continued to enjoy sewing when I had the time. My skills came in handy as I made curtains and fashioned slipcovers for the hand-me-down furniture we had in our first home. When the babies came along, I was overjoyed to be a stay-at-home mom. There wasn't much time to sew, but I made a few dresses for Kelli and crafted Halloween costumes for Matt. When I returned to the classroom as a kindergarten teacher, managing parenthood and full time teaching left room for little else.

There was a time, however, when my sewing skills were useful in the classroom. During the 1990s there was a trend in education based on research that showed students learned better in a welcoming environment. Teachers brought in plants, comfy chairs, and area rugs to make their classrooms feel "homey." I made curtains for my classroom, finding that a swath of color added much needed softness to the institutional bank of windows. It was a tradition that I continued throughout my career until my last year as a kindergarten teacher.

I had already made the train-themed curtains for my classroom that year. The educational trend had gone from comfy-cozy-classrooms to safety-first. School officials deemed that comfortable chairs and area rugs were incubators for head lice. Plants and classroom pets contributed to allergies. The principal told us she would allow curtains, but we had to coat them with a fireproofing spray. I complied and congratulated myself on how my room was coming together. But it wasn't to be.

"Due to fire marshal guidelines, curtains will *not* be allowed in classrooms," the memo commanded.

I took down the curtains, vowing to colleagues that I would make an outfit out of the fireproof, choo-choo curtains and wear it to the next staff meeting in protest. If a fire broke out during the meeting, I'd have an advantage.

Since I'd retired, I didn't have to worry about fire marshals. I could sew whatever I wanted. That's what I was thinking when the article about the Christmas pillowcases caught my eye. With the holidays coming up, it was the perfect project to help me brush up on my sewing skills. Off to the fabric store I went with the exact measurements in hand, eager to get started. The first pillowcase was a cute little reindeer print with a snowflake border. It stitched together in a flash and I ran to Ed's office to show off the finished product, eager to impress him with my talent.

"Look what I made!" I bragged.

"Wow," he said looking up from the computer. "That's nice."

Encouraged by the ease of my success, I trotted back to my sewing machine to stitch up another one. The candy cane print with red checked trim was delightful. As I snipped the last thread, I ran to Ed's office to reveal my latest creation. He wasn't there, but I tracked him down in the living room.

"Here's another one!" I beamed. "See how I made French seams so that the edges are nice and neat on the inside!"

"Mmm, yeah... that's great." He glanced away from the television, hardly noticing my exquisite French seams.

By the time I had finished the third pillowcase Ed was not in the office or living room. I found him in the bathroom. I'm sure he was hiding from me. That's when I realized I had a pillowcase addiction. The truth hit me hard. Convincing myself that I could quit at any time, I packed up the three pillowcases and shipped them off to my granddaughters. OK, I'll admit, I couldn't just quit cold turkey. I made two more of the darling cases and sent them to kids I barely knew.

The pillowcases were out of my system, but I couldn't quit thinking about sewing projects. My attention turned to aprons, then tote bags of different sizes and shapes. I signed up for sewing classes and pursued my dream of designing and sewing some of my clothing.

This fresh surge of creativity opened other avenues. The countless photos I took on our recent trip to England provided the perfect raw material to explore photo journaling as I documented our trip. Through this, I rekindled my love of writing. I'd considered myself to be a writer ever since my second grade teacher awarded me first place in the class poetry contest and put my poem outside in the hallway with a blue ribbon on it. I still remember it to this day:

Fire is hot
But snow is not.

Ok, I'll admit the competition among my fellow seven-year-old classmates must have been weak. Even so, I can claim to be an award-winning author from a young age.

My poetry fascination continued through my elementary school years. I uncovered a book of my poems in a box of paperwork that my mother had kept. On the first page, laboriously penciled in my fourth grade cursive writing it states: This book was written by Debra Joan Bennett. Copyright 1964.

Perusing its ancient pages I found this masterpiece:

Fish

I love to watch the fish swim 'round.
They have no feet to touch the ground.
Never eating from a dish.
And there off with one little swish.

My grammar needed work, but I was making progress. Moving on from there, my seventh grade science report on Mars earned top marks.

"Well written!" the red ink at the top of the page declared. "I liked the way you started off by grabbing the reader's attention with 'The Martians are coming! The Martians are coming!' from Orson Welles *War of the Worlds*."

Throughout my life, I'd turned to writing to express myself and record observations. I kept a detailed journal of my first year of motherhood, recording the changes I saw in my newborn daughter each day: her first smile, the day she rolled over, her first steps. I wanted to remember every detail of those precious moments.

Years later I wrote a story about a church trip to North Carolina. My husband, son, and I helped rebuild housing in an area that had experienced massive flood damage. It was a moving experience to work side by side with my now grown son as we labored to build a retaining wall around one property. I was elated when our denomination's national magazine accepted my story. Woo hoo! I was a published writer! But after editors rejected other stories, I became discouraged. Convinced I had no talent or at least lacked the confidence to handle a few slights, I put my writing aside and focused on my teaching career.

Months after I retired, I began to write again. It was a way for me to occupy my time and sort through the emotions I was feeling in my newfound life. I happened upon a writer's forum and attended their weekly meetings at the local library. I devoted time each day to my writing. Bit by bit my skill level improved, and I gained confidence in my abilities.

These writing and sewing projects and the communities I discovered around them were keeping me occupied and filling a need to engage my mind in creative, challenging, and social endeavors. I also found the work to be satisfying and inherently different from teaching. After spending a morning working on a poem, story, or sewing project, I had something tangible to show for my efforts.

In my teaching profession, though the goals were noble and the rewards great, it often took weeks, months, or even years to see progress. If I make a mistake sewing a garment or am not happy with the way a story is going, I can rip out seams and rewrite paragraphs. Struggling students were much harder to figure out. Many times solutions weren't obvious and it took many tries to succeed. There were times I wasn't able to unravel their tangled threads or smooth out their life stories.

So why did I stick with teaching for all those years? Because sometimes, sometimes, a spark ignites, a plan works, a struggling student smiles and succeeds, I made a difference, I reaped what I'd sewn. These moments, brief as they may be, are the rocket fuel that drives those of us who were and are fortunate enough to be educators. That passion drives me still. What direction it takes remains to be seen.

It was time to make space for my new life. As a first step, I repurposed my office where traces of my last years of teaching piled up in the corners, closet, and bookshelves. It was a therapeutic process to go through stacks of teachers' guides, evaluations, planning books, and children's books that had been a crucial part of my life. The process helped me define what I no longer needed and what I would carry forward.

I positioned a small writing desk to face the window where I can gaze out over our Southwestern garden and view the Catalina Mountains. White pegboard hangs on one wall to hold my sewing supplies and a framed picture of my mother smiles down on me. Underneath the pegboard unit, a fold-down craft table displays my faithful 1970s Sears Kenmore sewing machine, ready to hum to life when inspiration strikes.

On my bookshelf I placed some mementos of my long teaching career: a small wooden sign that reads *Best Teacher Ever,* a ceramic red apple with a golden leaf and stem engraved with my name, a collection of my favorite children's books, and a bright yellow stuffed Star-Bellied-Sneetch from a Dr. Seuss story. A picture featuring my trio of granddaughters has a place of honor on the top shelf. Their ebony, gold, and strawberry hair intertwine as they lie in the grass on a bright summer morning, reminding me they are growing up way too fast. I reserved some shelves for my expanding collection of books by authors that inspire me and I have space for the journals I'm filling. A seldom used set of watercolor paints on the bottom shelf is tempting me.

It's a cozy space. I can imagine spending lots of time here pursuing my creative life. There are seams to sew and stories to weave. But just to make sure I don't get too complacent, I've decorated the walls with posters and pictures of our trip to England and a picture of Ed holding my hand as we walk along a beach. Little reminders to nudge me into the world to collect new stories and inspirations.

I was ready to get to work. There was just one more box to go through.

Report Card

The tattered cardboard box had traveled far. It had survived many moves and now stood in a corner of a spare closet with an assortment of other things I intended to go through *some* day. Someday was now.

With a sigh, I pulled the box from the closet. My mother's handwriting scrawled across the top of the box announcing the contents as *Debbie's School Papers*. I'm not sure when Mom had passed the box on to me. I'd sifted through the contents from time to time, wondering why she would keep such silly things. When I became a mother I understood. I'd passed on similar collections to my children when they started off on their own.

I peeked inside. CLEAR CREEK KINDERGARTEN, 1970-1971, was neatly lettered in black marker on the faded blue cover of a scrapbook. The pages were yellowed and brittle with age. It took me back to my senior year in high school in Bloomington, Indiana. I signed up for the cadet teaching class that year because I'd finished my core requirements for graduation and thought it would be an effortless way to finish up my last semester of high school. As a cadet teacher, I would work in an elementary classroom to see if I might be interested in a career in teaching.

Each morning I drove to my assigned school and helped in the kindergarten class. What started out as a way to coast through senior year turned into a love affair. I fell in love with kindergarten. Story time on the rug, playdough, puppets, and the way Soundie the magical elf brought a new letter to learn each week, all of it. It seemed like play to me, and I wanted to learn more about how young children learned. When the semester ended, the students made a scrapbook for me by writing thank-you notes and drawing pictures. One of my favorites shows Miss Bennett, my professional name in those days, leading the class down the hallway. The artist had attached my circle head to a T-shaped body and I'm towering above the students on stick legs. Five smiling, stick-figure students line up behind me.

The dictated note reads:

Dear Miss Bennett,
I like for you to read us stories. Thank you for helping us with letters and numbers. Thank you for taking us to the gym. We will have a surprise for you tomorrow!
Blaine

Blaine and the other Clear Creek kindergarteners had a profound effect on my life. As the year progressed, I became invested in these five-year-olds. I came to know them as individuals with unique personalities, interests, and needs. I saw how a teacher could make a difference. It was this cadet teaching experience that prompted me to pursue a college degree in elementary education with a kindergarten endorsement and later, a master's degree in Early Childhood Education. I would spend more than half of my career in kindergarten classrooms.

I put the fragile scrapbook back together and laid it aside. Further into the keepsake box, I discovered my first grade report card from Poston Road School in Martinsville, Indiana, dated 1959-1960. My parents, younger brother, and I lived with my grandparents for part of that year. Poston Road was a neighborhood school within walking distance of my grandparent's house. With no cafeteria service, students brought a sack lunch or walked home for lunch. I have fond memories of eating lunch with my grandparents before heading back to school for the afternoon. To this day, grilled cheese sandwiches and tomato soup are my go-to comfort foods. On frigid winter days, it was hard to leave the safety and warmth of that kitchen.

As I pulled the ancient report card out of its envelope, I saw an assortment of checks and pluses for reading, writing, spelling, and arithmetic. The top of the card caught my attention. Under the title "Habits and Attitudes" I came across the category "Refrains from disturbing others." I got a plus for this. The wording of this phrase struck me as odd. The term *refrains* makes it appear I *wanted* to disturb others or *should* have disturbed others, but I restrained myself. Even stranger to me, the score of "plus" indicates my teacher had assessed I was above average in the skill of holding back. Sadly, what Mrs. Clarisey saw as self-control was extreme shyness. I was a very timid child, afraid of my teachers, afraid to answer questions or stand out in any way.

My first grade reading book was in the box of memories. I learned to read stories about Dick, Jane, Sally, and their pets: Spot, the dog and Puff, the cat. Dick, with his shirt neatly tucked into his khaki shorts, and his sisters in their frilly dresses introduced me to my first words.

The teacher assigned us to reading groups based on our ability and gave each group a bird name: Cardinals, Blue Jays, and Wrens. When it was time to read, the designated birds picked up their small wooden chairs and flocked to the circle to join Mrs. Clarisey. We clutched our soft-covered books and read aloud, one by one, going around the circle. Years later, in my elementary education classes, I learned they called this "round robin" reading. Maybe *that's* why our reading groups had bird names.

It terrified me to read aloud. I tried my best to follow along, my shaky finger moving across the page as each student plodded along word by word. When it was my turn, my heart thumped, and I stumbled over words that I read effortlessly at home to my mother.

It would be many years before I gained the self-confidence I needed to become a teacher. Yet I still remember what it felt like to be that shy girl from Poston Road School. Later, in each of my classrooms, I looked for that child. He or she would be the student sitting quietly, following directions, trying their best, easily overlooked in a busy classroom where those who weren't "refraining from bothering others," commanded my attention.

It's interesting to note that the term "refrains from bothering others" from my 1960 report card did not appear on any of the report cards I filled out as a teacher. This terminology transformed into "Keeps hands and feet to self," a phrase that may still be a part of our education lingo today. Bless our hearts, but as educators we always try to put a positive spin on things. "Keeps hands and feet to self" sounds more positive on a report card than "Hits, pushes, and kicks others," a more precise description of the behavior we are evaluating. Technically, "keeping your hands and feet to yourself" only applies to hands and feet. Arguably, other body parts are free to do as they please.

There were many times in my career when students with behavior issues would demand more than their fair share of my attention. Other times, I would be charmed by the popular kids— bubbly, cute, and chatty. But often, I would get a nudge from my first-grade self.

"She's afraid. She's never been away from home. Give her time to adjust."

It was the first day of kindergarten. With the help of my teacher assistant, Judy, my students put their new school supplies into their cubbies and made their way to the rug in the center of the room. Sophie hid under a table. The separation from her mother had been abrupt. Sophie released her mother's leg, and the tears had stopped, but this was as close to us as Sophie would get. My strategy was to give her space and let her observe us for a while.

When I got the class settled in, I took out my guitar and sang *Here We Are Together,* my traditional welcome to kindergarten. We sang the cheery melody as we added in each student's name. When I got to Sophie's name, several students turned to stare at the child huddled under the table.

After the song ended, I gave a few simple directions for the activity we would do next.

"Are there any questions?" I asked.

"Why's that girl under the table?" Dylan blurted out.

All eyes were on Sophie.

"Boys and girls," I said gently, "our friend Sophie just needs some time to get used to kindergarten. I'm sure she'll join us once she sees how much fun we're having."

"Well," Dylan grumbled, "It hasn't been that much fun so far."

I was sorry the first few moments of kindergarten didn't live up to Dylan's expectations.

It took time for Sophie to make the transition to school. I understood. Facing unfamiliar circumstances can be terrifying. Even as a teacher I would get butterflies in my stomach on the first day of each new year. But bit by bit, Sophie learned to trust that our classroom would be a safe place where she could take her first steps towards independence.

Many years later, the voice from my past was still instructing me.

"There, that one. Help him find his voice."

Daniel was a student in my fourth grade class. Gifted and bright, he came from a professional family that valued achievement. We had been working hard on our independent science projects and it was time for Daniel to share with the class. He'd done his research, and I looked forward to an amazing presentation. Daniel crept to the front of the class and projected his first slide. The class waited for him to begin, but Daniel stood rigid with his back to the class and his eyes on the ground in front of him. Several silent moments passed by. I held my breath, and Daniel's classmates fidgeted in their seats. From my position at the front of the class, I heard his voice muttering over the hum of the projector, "I have failed, I have failed."

My heart was breaking.

Unsure of what to do, I softly read the words on the slide. Daniel looked up and whispered along with me. It was shaky, but together we got through the first slide, then the second. After the third slide, I quit reading and Daniel's voice carried on alone. As he finished, the class burst into applause. Only then did Daniel turn and face his audience. A hint of a smile flickered across his face as he ducked his head, hurrying back to the safety of his seat.

I knew I had just witnessed a major act of courage as Daniel overcame the fear that had paralyzed him. I hoped he would carry this moment with him as a source of strength the next time he faced an audience. So often, the arena of teaching wasn't about the subject matter I taught, but about the life lessons I shared with my students. That day I had a front-row seat.

So, how do you sum up a career? Was I satisfied with my life's work? How would I measure my success? I still had my professional evaluations from the last three years of teaching. Unlike my first-grade report card neatly tucked into a small, manila envelope, this "teacher report card" was a stack of paperwork taking up the entire corner of the closet. It amounted to several years of pre- and post-observation notes and rubric scores that boiled down to a single number summing up my professional skills.

I'm not sure why I had saved this mountain of paperwork. Did I think someone might show up on my doorstep one day and demand to see proof that I had been a successful teacher? Was I afraid if I couldn't provide the proper documentation, they might strip me of my retirement status and deport me back into the classroom? Perhaps my heirs would discover the documents one day after I was long gone and claim, "Wow! Look at Grandma's scores in *uses multiple means to engage students!*" Or maybe, just maybe, I thought the score was me, a number that summed up thirty-seven years of teaching, and I was afraid to let go of it. It was a noble number, and I had worked hard for it, but is this how I wanted to measure my career? What to hold on to and what to let go of?

I debated for just a moment before making my decision. I picked up the stack of teacher evaluations and pitched it in the trash. This made plenty of room in the closet for the scrapbook the kindergarten students at Clear Creek Elementary made for me during my cadet teaching experience in 1971.

Five decades later I look back on the picture of stick-legged Miss Bennett, leading her little group of students. I see myself as a young woman on the brink of a journey of a lifetime. Along the way I would meet Blaine, Sophie, Daniel and hundreds of other students, parents, and colleagues. Together we faced challenges and celebrated triumphs. I was privileged to have had the opportunity to help my students with their own journeys, sending them off at the end of each year knowing that I had made a difference. It has been an amazing adventure.

I set out to be a teacher, but I realize now that I also became a student. With each new encounter I learned more about myself and what I am capable of. Through my journey I discovered that I am smart, creative, resilient, hardworking, sensitive, resourceful, positive-thinking... and just the right amount of crazy. My retirement from teaching doesn't change that. Maybe this is what I was searching for as I sifted through the box in the closet. I look back on my career with pride and satisfaction. This is the "report card" I will carry with me for the next part of my life.

Real Life

With my office/studio in order, I was ready to write some stories about my teaching career.

I thought about the crazy pollywogs I'd encountered during my first year of teaching kindergarten. Fresh out of college, I'd learned that young children need real-life experiences with their world. I asked my students to search the creeks and ponds surrounding their homes and bring in any tadpoles they found. When a mason jar of mucky pond water and wiggly black dots showed up on my desk the next day, I was ecstatic. We could now observe the metamorphosis from tadpole to frog firsthand.

The class helped me set up a small aquarium filled with a slight amount of pond water. We placed stones around one side anticipating the time when our tadpoles developed from underwater gill breathers to land-loving frogs. We made a chart and took turns putting a pinch of fish food in the water each day. It didn't take long before tiny back legs sprouted on the babies.

Something else was happening in the aquarium. Two of the tadpoles had dappled green bodies and grew much faster than the others. Feathery gills fanned out from the sides of their heads causing them to resemble the Creature from the Black Lagoon. I noticed the smaller, dark tadpoles were mysteriously disappearing. I explained it away by telling the class that it's hard to keep wild creatures in captivity. Maybe we didn't keep the pond water fresh enough, or we weren't feeding them the right food, but I had other suspicions. The two large tadpoles thrived. Soon they were the only tadpoles left in the aquarium. After doing some research, we discovered they weren't frog larvae; these tadpoles would be turning into salamanders. The class named them Polly and Wog.

One morning I arrived early and began setting up the classroom for the day. I peeked into the aquarium. To my horror, I saw Polly, having apparently eaten the last of the little black tadpoles, now attempting to swallow Wog head first. He struggled to back out of Polly's mouth creating a gruesome battle of life and death. A muffled scream escaped my throat. My students would arrive any minute. I couldn't expose my darling five-year-olds to a display of amphibian cannibalism. I grabbed the aquarium and ran to the field behind the playground. In one quick move, I flipped the aquarium over and heaved its watery contents to the ground. Now the conjoined salamanders fought a different battle as their gills flailed in and out trying to breathe unfamiliar air. I knew they would soon be dead, but I didn't care. I returned to the school, clutching the empty aquarium, and tried to erase the sight of the writhing salamanders from my mind.

When the class asked about the missing tadpoles I said I'd turned them loose. It wasn't a lie.

Years later, still on a mission to bring nature into the classroom, I set up a fish aquarium. Through trial and error, I found goldfish to be an excellent option: inexpensive, low maintenance, and hardy. Occasionally one would expire. When this happened, I would dip it out, fold it into a paper towel and drop it into the trash can before the students arrived. I would replace it the next day with a brand new fish, thus creating the illusion of eternal life in Aquarium World.

One morning, I noticed a fish floating belly-up at the top of the aquarium. I grabbed the net and made a last-minute decision to flush the fish down the toilet instead of my usual trash can disposal method. Scoop, run, plop, flush. Just in time. When my students arrived, I began our morning as if nothing had happened. I almost got by with it. Until 8:45 when Joel had to go potty.

"Ahhhhhhhh!" The startled boy came screaming out of the bathroom. "I peed in the toilet and then... and then there was a fish in there!"

Utter chaos erupted as every five-year-old in the class raced to the bathroom to see the fish in the toilet. It took myself and two teacher assistants to get everyone back to the story-time rug and calmed down. My students looked at me for an explanation. I considered lying. I could say the fish accidentally jumped out of the tank, found the nearest water source, and climbed into the toilet. There's a chance that they'd believe my story. Most still had faith in Santa Claus, the Easter Bunny, and the Tooth Fairy, but I realized I had to tell them the truth.

"The thing is..." I began, "when I came in this morning I found Goldie floating at the top of the aquarium. He wasn't alive. I flushed him down the toilet, but I guess his body floated back up. I'm sorry. It was a terrible idea."

The class forgave me. However, they let me know that we couldn't leave Goldie floating in Joel's pee. They solemnly stood by while I scooped the fish out with the net. We buried him in the flower bed outside our classroom door and conducted a simple funeral service for him. No, he wouldn't sprout back to life like the seeds we planted there earlier.

Decades had passed and the pollywogs and goldfish stories were on my mind. I thought they were funny anecdotes and I couldn't wait to share them with my writing group.

"This would make a cute story," a friend said, "but why did you think you had to shield your students from death? What's the *real* story here?"

My fragile writer's ego was crushed, but I knew she was right. I was in my sixth decade, and I still struggled with the hard truths of life. I preferred to live my life in happy moments, glossing over any rough parts. But I knew that if I wanted to grow as a writer and, more importantly as a person, I would have to go deeper. Like going through that old tattered box in my storage closet, I would need to reach in to my psyche and pull some things out for a closer look.

My feelings about death were rooted in my upbringing. My mother believed in protecting children from the unpleasantries of life; Dad favored a more realistic approach. This difference in philosophy revealed itself when we played Monopoly. Dad played to win. If we landed on one of his loaded properties and couldn't pay the rent, Mom would slip us money under the table so we wouldn't go bankrupt.

"Alice, stop doing that," he'd say. "They have to learn about the real world sometime."

"It's a game, Jack. It's not intended to make children cry."

No one died in Monopoly. We might run out of money and be out of the game, but with Mom around, we never had to face that possibility.

I grew up in the everlasting fish bowl where no one died, got sick, or had problems. Certainly my family experienced these things, but we never discussed such matters around the dinner table. My parents lovingly tucked me in each night reciting, "Now I lay me down to sleep..." quickly mumbling the "If I die before I wake..." part. I sometimes heard snippets of my parents' hushed conversations after us kids went to bed. Perhaps that's when they discussed real-life issues. I'm guessing not.

There's a family photo that's always been a favorite of mine. My mother keeps it on a shelf in her room in her memory care community. I have a copy as well. The professional, black and white photo was the first family photo for Mom and Dad taken when I was around six months old. I'm sitting on top of a table; my parents stand behind me, only visible from the waist up. Everyone is smiling. It's a beautiful picture.

My dad, smart and handsome, is at the beginning of his professional journey. His arms are at his side, hands hidden under the table. His dark suit and the boldly striped, fashionable tie exude his emerging professionalism, yet his crooked, boyish grin indicates a playful side that he is trying to hide behind his stiff clothes and rigid posture. His suit is new and slightly too big for him like he hasn't quite grown into his professional role.

My mother, beautiful and stylish, tilts her head slightly towards Dad. Her smile indicates openness and warmth. One arm rests on the table, the other is supporting me, behind my back. She has overcome much and is proud of where she is now. Her careful attention to her looks, clothing, and jewelry show that she is ready to take on her role of a supportive wife of a professional man. My parents take on equal importance in the photo, Mom isn't dwarfed by her husband though he is taller. Theirs would be a marriage of equals.

I take my spot in this family photo, center stage as my parents' first born. I wear a crisp white dress, all ruffles and bows. I am a blend of them both. I have Dad's lopsided smile, mom's eyes, and nose. Mom and I have matching curls over our ears. My fancy dress and perfectly combed hair show that appearances are important to this family, yet I'm wearing sturdy walking shoes. I like this. It seems to be saying to the world that I'm eager to get going. I have one arm raised, my baby fist clenched in a "Rosie the Riveter" pose. If you substitute my baby fat for arm muscle, I have an attitude of "Let's do this!"

All of the faces in the photo are happy; that's how I remember my childhood. Happy. Secure. Sheltered. I was shocked to learn that life isn't always happy.

I must have been seven or eight years old when I had my first encounter with death. It was Mom's birthday. We'd just finished dinner when our neighbor called.

"Oh no," Mom whispered into the mouthpiece of the harvest-gold, wall-mounted phone. "I'll send Jack up right away."

A car had hit our dog, Princess. I ran to the window. The orange glow of the streetlight made the softly falling snow look like Mother Nature was sprinkling glitter to cover up the broken brown shape lying in the fresh car tracks. I wondered if there was blood in the snow. I turned away as my dad put on his coat and hat. When I try to recall more details of that night, I find the golden glitter has buried painful emotions creating holes in my memory. Did I cry? What did my dad do with Princess' body? What did my parents say to us? When my memory returns me to the scene, I'm watching television in the den with Dad and my brother and sister while mom is washing the dinner dishes. I remember feeling a deep sadness for my mother. Doing dishes by herself... on her birthday... on the day the dog died... as if nothing had happened.

When I became a parent, I tried to prepare my children better. One day four-year-old Kelli came running into my bedroom.

"Mommy, something's wrong with Bucky! Come look."

She took my hand and led me to the fish aquarium. Indeed, there was something wrong with Bucky. He'd perished during the night and the other fish had consumed him leaving nothing but a fish skeleton at the bottom of the tank. Rather than whisking the remains away, we stayed a while to observe the little pile of bones. I started the delicate conversation.

"Honey, Bucky is... *I took a gulp...* dead."

There, I did it. I said the "d" word.

We had been attending church and Bible study classes. I relied on my newfound theology and explained that Bucky wouldn't be able to swim around anymore. To soften the blow, I told her that God had taken him to heaven, a special fish heaven. That seemed to make sense to her, and she ran downstairs to play with her collection of "My Little Ponies." A few minutes later she trotted back and asked,

"Mommy, why didn't God take his bones?"

That was a little harder for me to explain. I did my best to relate what I believed about fish souls leaving their bodies.

"Bucky doesn't need his bones anymore," I'd said.

"But Mommy, how's Bucky going to swim around in God's 'quarium without his bones?"

Shortly after the Bucky experience, my grandfather died. At thirty years old, I had never been to a funeral home or seen a dead body. I stood at the casket expecting to find Grandpa. He was dressed in his best navy blue suit with his hands folded serenely on his tummy. A fancy pillow supported his head. With his eyes closed he looked like he might have just been sleeping, but the frozen face and fake smile gave it away. Scores of people walked by to say goodbye to him. Didn't they know he'd already left?

I now understood what dead meant. I would no longer see his eyes twinkle when he told a silly joke, no longer hear his voice call me "Sweetie Pie," or feel his scratchy whiskers on my face when he kissed my cheek. Grandpa used to let me ride with him in his Johnson's milk truck as he made deliveries to local grocery stores. He fixed grilled cheese and tomato soup when I came home from first grade for lunch and made the best hot cocoa on a cold winter morning.

Grandpa was born on Halloween and it was his favorite holiday. He taught me how to carve a pumpkin, taking care to slice the top around the stem by angling the knife so that the top wouldn't slip back into the pumpkin shell. Then we'd scoop out the seeds using his favorite ice cream scooper. With his pocket knife, Grandpa carved the eyes, nose, and mouth. As we put the special star-shaped candle holder in the bottom of the pumpkin and lit the candle, our pumpkin turned into a Jack-o'-lantern. When Grandpa joked about how his parents named him Jack, in honor of the holiday, his mouth turned up on the corners reminding me of the face we had just created.

Now, Grandpa's essence, his soul, had gone, leaving behind an empty shell. The pain of it shook me to my core. I needed to know that it wasn't the end, that there would be a part of Grandpa for me to hold on to. I understood now why my parents tried to shelter me as long as possible. Death can swoop down and uproot us, changing our world in seconds, leaving those left behind with questions and pain. I discovered that faith isn't just going to church and Bible study lessons. It became personal, a belief there is more to life than what we can explain.

I look once more at the family photo. I want to tell the baby girl that she will be one of the lucky ones; the smiles in her life will far outnumber the tears. But, make no mistake, there will be times when sadness and grief will overcome her. When the tears come, she will gain strength from the people in her life that love her. And there will be many of those people. Sadness and happiness flow together in life. Tadpoles, fish and puppies die. Grandpas die. It's OK to cry. That's how she will know she is real.

And a real life challenge was about to present itself.

Lost and Found

This wasn't part of the plan. We'd retired six months ago expecting to go through our golden years together; now Ed was in the hospital. I'd been sitting alone in the outpatient waiting room all morning. Tense and worried, I needed a change of scenery. Besides, the trip to the cafeteria would help pass the time. With Ed in recovery, it would be several hours before I could take him home. I approached the volunteer behind the front desk for directions.

"Just follow the flower tiles on the floor. They should lead you right to your destination," the lady in the blue smock told me. "Be sure to take this so we can get in touch with you if we need to." She handed me a pager as if I was expecting a table to open up at Applebee's. I shoved the device into my purse, afraid that it may not be announcing such wonderful news.

I've never been good with directions. I have a diploma from Fairview Kindergarten and a Master's degree from Indiana University, but I still can't do left and right. If you ask me to make a specific directional turn while driving, I'll hesitate while my brain makes a calculation. I might even sneak the hand I write with off the wheel for an instant and clutch a pretend pencil. Right hand. Yep, turn this way. I blame it on my second-grade teacher. In her class, students sat in straight rows facing the teacher's desk. During our morning exercises, we stood beside our desks and Mrs. Mitchell would say, "Remember, your right side is towards the window." As long as I was in her class I had no problem, but now that I am outside that second-grade classroom, who knows which way the windows are? There's no point of reference. I maintain it's not my fault I'm directionally challenged. Knowing this, it isn't surprising I got lost that day.

At first, following the cheerful flowers through the many twists and turns in the corridor seemed easy. It reminded me of the shapes I'd taped to the rug in kindergarten to show my students where to sit. Soon I saw the sign for the cafeteria and passed through the double doors. The room, in the hospital's center, had no view of the outside world. Landscape murals, a neutral color palette, and soft music conspired to create a tranquil atmosphere. It wasn't working on me.

I glanced at the hot-food area where hair-netted employees stood over steaming trays of mushy main courses. In my state of anxiety, the smells emanating from that part of the cafeteria nauseated me. Looking for lighter fare, I found a "grab and go" section where I selected a turkey sandwich accessorized with a ruffle of limp lettuce. On the way to check out, I picked up a bag of chips and a soft drink. There was a lengthy row of hospital staff waiting to pay, and I was almost to the register when I saw the "employees only" sign. With a sigh, I trudged to the end of the guest line.

After paying, I found a table for one. Placing the pager by my tray, I settled into my space. I hate eating by myself. With a shiver, I hoped this wasn't a preview of things to come. I nibbled on my sandwich and watched the other diners. A group of hospital employees laughed and chatted while at the next table a family conversed in somber tones. The contrast between the two groups was stark. I picked at my food, finding I had little appetite. Giving up on my meal, I tossed the remains in the trash bin. I was anxious to get back to my post in the waiting room.

Following a group of blue-clad workers into the hallway, I searched for the flowered tiles, but they'd vanished. Did I come out a different door? After a few false starts, I stood in the Alice-in-wonderland maze feeling as if I'd ingested the contents of the "Drink Me" bottle. Where were those flowers? My imagination got the best of me, and I feared I'd walk into an operating room by accident. I pictured myself entering a sterile room; the only light coming from an industrial light fixture hanging over a draped patient.

"Get that woman out of here!" The gowned and masked doctor would shriek.

The thought of what I might see on the steel table made me weak in the knees.

With a sinking feeling, I realized I was lost. Not just disoriented by the confusing array of hallways and doors, but terrified of being lost forever. What if the cancer was worse than the doctor expected? Maybe Ed wouldn't make it. Would I spend the rest of my life wandering around alone and wondering which way to turn?

My clouded mind sabotaged any attempts I made to get my bearings. No one showed up to rescue me, and I wandered for what seemed like an eternity. Just as I thought it hopeless, I saw a flower... then another and another. My steps quickened. As I pushed through a familiar set of double doors, the outpatient waiting room greeted me like an old friend.

I let out a sigh of relief and settled into the nearest vinyl-covered chair. The television mounted to the wall ran a loop of exercise and health tips that no one watched. While others gathered in pairs, trios and quartets, I was solo. Though I'd phoned updates to my family throughout the morning, they seemed far away now. While searching my bag for something to read, my fingers found the soft texture of a prayer shawl that I'd tucked in at the last moment. A friend had knitted it for me years ago when I was recovering from a nasty fall. The warmth of the yarn provided a much-needed hug as it draped around my shoulders. A book sat unopened on my lap and I fidgeted with my wedding ring. Ed removed his before going into surgery. I checked my purse again to make sure the band was there.

When we became engaged in 1973, we wanted our rings to be unique. Argentum Jewelers in Bloomington, Indiana specialized in custom work and their shop was next to my grandparent's bakery where I had a summer job. We worked with the artist to design a beautiful two-piece set for me. White-gold leaves and vines wrap around the band and lead up to a flower that supports a small but brilliant diamond. Ed had surprised me with the engagement ring at his grandmother's house that Christmas. It has seldom left my finger. His band complimented the vine theme. It was important to keep it safe. Yes, please be safe. The ring, and the man who wore it, were irreplaceable.

A pulsating sound and a circle of flashing lights coming from the pager interrupted my thoughts. I sprang out of my seat, sending the device clattering to the floor. Others glanced up and gave me a quick nod as I walked to the reception desk. Their eyes met mine and mirrored the anxiety I felt. They too, were poised, wondering when their alarms would go off and what news they would receive. The blue-smocked lady silenced the device and led me to the conference area where the surgeon would see me. I fought back tears, hoping for the best.

The news was good, Stage Zero, meaning the cancer hadn't spread. The doctor was confident he'd gotten it all and was optimistic that Ed would have a full recovery. We were to call his office the next morning and schedule an appointment to discuss follow-up treatment options. Seeing the tears sliding down my face, he put his hand on my shoulder and said, "We've got this. It will be Ok."

That evening Ed and I sat on our back porch facing the Catalina Mountains in the Arizona home we'd grown to love. Ominous clouds blocked the sunlight, and the mountains wore a somber shade of ash. As if on cue, the sun broke through and flooded the sky with color. Once-gray clouds exploded into a blaze of flamingo fluff. Peaks and valleys became alive and vibrant rays turned slate into gold.

Without words, we knew we had been given a gift. It was not yet time for us to say goodbye to each other. There would be opportunities for quiet everyday moments and glorious adventures together, but it had been a close call. We dared not take a single minute for granted.

We phoned family members to let them know things would be all right; we'd be able to go back east and join them for the Christmas holiday as planned. As the sun sank lower in the sky and turned the mountains to sienna, we got a wild thought. Our next call was to our travel buddies, Ann and Scott.

"Hey, let's start planning that trip to Italy we've been dreaming about."

La Dolce Vita

Ciao

Ten months later, we were driving through the Tuscan countryside outside of Florence. While Ed got acquainted with the rented Volvo, Ann called out directions from the passenger seat. Rather than booking a scheduled group tour of Italy, we'd made our own plans for accommodations, transportation, and activities. We wanted to stay away from the tourist traps as much as possible to create a more authentic experience and had booked a fifteenth century villa for the week. As we left the city behind, the landscape unfolded before my eyes. The sunlight cast a golden glow on the hillsides, brushing the olive groves, vineyards, and cypress trees as if a Renaissance painter had created them. After a hectic morning of travel, I relaxed and let myself sink into the scenery, worlds away from my life as a teacher.

We found a quaint cafe in a tiny village perched on the side of a hill and stopped for lunch. A deli case brimming with meats and cheeses dominated the cozy space. Loaves of baked bread lined the counter, and a display of local wines filled the shelves. A few locals sat at scattered tables and gave us a quick look before returning to their conversations. We hesitated, unsure whether we should wait to be seated. A young lady greeted us.

"Buongiorno!"

"Lunch?" I asked.

"Si, si." She smiled as she gathered menus and showed us to a small wooden table for four. Ordering from the Italian menu was an adventure in teamwork and creativity.

"Focaccia and ciabatta are both breads. Is this a sandwich?"

"I think 'Parma' is a type of ham."

"Pecorino? Is that like pepperoni?"

"No, it's cheese."

The language barrier made it impossible to order with confidence, so we went with Plan B: pointing to items in the deli case. The man behind the counter grinned as he sliced off hunks of dried meats, bread, and cheese and poured tall glasses of Chianti.

"Salute!" We clinked our goblets together and welcomed ourselves to Tuscany.

From the cafe, it was a short drive to our villa. We stopped at the ornate iron gate where our host, Sylvie, greeted us with hugs and escorted our group up the gravel path bordered with Cyprus trees. Our excitement grew as the three-story structure revealed itself, its ochre-hued exterior and red- tiled roof nestled in the lush landscape. We would have the entire first floor of the villa. Although the two bed-two bath unit included a modern kitchen and air conditioning, there were many signs of the old structure. Craftsmen had painstakingly restored the frescos on the ancient walls and we walked on age-worn stone floors. The vaulted ceilings retained their intricate pattern of arches and designs. Wisps of white lace hung from the tall, deep windows that framed pristine views of the olive groves outside. I unpacked my bags and immediately felt at home.

Magnum opus

The decision to experience living in the Tuscan countryside meant we would embark on a perilous trek into Florence every morning for sightseeing. The steep road was barely wide enough for one car. When faced with oncoming traffic, both vehicles would stop and one would back up to find a suitable place to pull over. To add to the excitement, our GPS, when working, seemed to send us in a different direction each day. As we entered Florence, we merged with commuters dashing to work on bicycles, scooters and cars. I huddled in the backseat, not daring to look until at last we made it to the parking lot at a large grocery where we could catch the train into the city center.

In the heart of Florence, we mingled with elegantly dressed Italians and throngs of casually clad tourists. On our first day in the city, we planned to visit the Galleria Academia, home to Michelangelo's statue of David. Though we'd purchased our tickets months in advance, we waited in a long line outside the gallery. Once inside, we continued to be in a mass of sightseers inching their way to David at the end of the grand chamber.

As we got closer, the crowd fell silent and formed a circle around the seventeen-foot statue as if in the presence of a deity. I'd seen pictures, of course, but to encounter this masterpiece in person took my breath away. I was amazed that a piece of cold stone could hold such emotion and movement. We would later visit Rome, where we viewed his Pieta and the Sistine chapel, an amazing legacy from this Renaissance artist. I sat on a bench in the rotunda and gazed at the creation for quite some time. I was in awe of the talent, determination, and genius it had taken to bring marble to life.

Later that day we visited the Uffizi Gallery where we saw Botticelli's *Birth of Venus* and artwork by Leonardo da Vinci, Raphael and many others. Having been a high school English teacher, Scott led us on a walking tour of the city to retrace the steps of the poet Dante. Magnificent works of art of all types surrounded us. Though I'd never be an artist of this sort, their desire to create stirred me. Through sculpture, painting, and the written word, they'd left behind a life's work, a legacy.

On the drive back to the villa that evening, it occurred to me we all leave a legacy. What would be *my* legacy? My teaching career, marriage, parenthood, and grandparenting would play a major part, yet I had the feeling that there was more to come.

Buon Appetito

In pursuit of Italian masterpieces of a different nature, we signed up for a cooking class. On the day of the class, we gathered along with twenty other students in the center of Florence and met Maria, our guide and one of our two chefs for the day. After greetings and introductions, she led us to the city market where locals and restaurant owners went to shop each morning. In this bustling marketplace we sampled Italian cheeses: pecorino made with sheep's milk and served with a drizzle of local honey and Parmigiano-Reggiano, the hard cheese that is perfect for grating. Next, Maria took us to the meat counter where she selected freshly ground pork and beef for Bolognese sauce. The experience enchanted Ed, the head chef of our family. After days of looking at sculptures and paintings, he'd found his canvas. We had to drag him away.

It was a short walk from the market to the classroom where we took our seats at one of four marble-topped tables. Using the ingredients Maria had purchased, Chef Marco demonstrated how to make Bolognese with fresh tomato sauce. It wasn't long before savory aromas filled the air.

Now it was time for class participation. We were going to be making our own pasta to go with the sauce that was bubbling away in the front of the room. True to Italian custom, we would make the pasta from scratch. Marco dumped a measure of flour on the marble table top.

"Next, we make a well in the flour like this," he instructed. "Then crack one egg in the center and begin to work the flour in slowly, being careful not to break the sides of the well."

Using a fork, he incorporated the egg into the flour until a pale yellow lump of dough formed.

"Now you try," he said as assistant chefs brought flour and eggs to each table. I glanced across the table at Scott who was much more comfortable with Dante than with dough.

"Nothing I do here will turn out right," he muttered, staring at the mound of flour on the table in front of him. He was more of a 'sandwich chef' at home, leaving most of the cooking to Ann. I turned my attention to my own work, carefully breaking an egg in the middle of my flour nest and stirring in the flour. To my pleasure, the dough formed just as expected.

"Ok, next we roll the dough." We gathered around Marco's table as he floured the marble surface and formed the dough into a perfect rectangle. I was confident about this step. It looked like the pie dough I used to make. We returned to our tables to continue.

"Good, good. Just a bit thinner," the chef commented as he approached me. I basked in the light of being the star pupil.

Though Ann was cautioned against using too much flour ("No more flour for you!"), she and Ed were making good progress and Scott was proceeding with help. Several in the class had failed to make the dough correctly and had to start over.

Feeling smug, I continued to roll my dough as I watched the remedial students. As Marco made his rounds, I anticipated another compliment.

"Oh Madame, you have gone too far!" he said as he looked at what I was doing. "Students, students, you mustn't roll it too thin or it will end up like this. Madame, you must start over."

I was crushed. I was used to being the teacher, the one in charge, the one who got things right. After a few embarrassing giggles, and a sip of wine, I let go of the need to be perfect and gave myself permission to fail, permission to be a student. It was a refreshing perspective. As the lumps of dough transformed into strips of pasta, I added mine to the platter in the center of the table. When all the platters were full, Maria and Marco whisked them away to the kitchen to cook. We refilled our wine glasses and chatted with the Canadian couple who'd shared our table. Soon we were dining on plates of imperfect pasta with

Bolognese sauce and thoroughly enjoying ourselves. At the end of class Marco and Maria presented us with diplomas that read:

Diamante Academy
Certificate of Proficiency
In Italian Cuisine

As we said our goodbyes and prepared to leave, Ed wasn't with us. I turned and found him sitting at the table having a serious conversation with Marco.

"NO, NO, *never* put cream in carbonara," the chef retorted.

Ed was already thinking about his next masterpiece. I looked forward to flour-and-egg-smeared countertops at home and the memories we would share. Saturday night dinners would never be the same.

La Grande Avventura

When we were planning our trip to Italy, Ann came across an interesting online advertisement:

Tour the Tuscan wine country by Vespa!
Light lunch and wine included!

What a ridiculous thought. Imagine the four of us zipping around on scooters. When the laughter died down, I thought for a moment.

"Why not?" I challenged. "We want this trip to be an adventure. We're over sixty after all; this may be our last chance to do something wild." I could already picture myself riding through Italy, Audrey Hepburn style, in large sunglasses with my scarf blowing behind me. After much debate, we booked the tickets. When he heard our plans, my son Matt was less than enthused.

"Mom, this isn't like riding a bicycle; a Vespa is a motorized machine. You've never driven anything like this before."

"That's the whole point," I explained as I dismissed his concerns. Besides, the information on the site said they would provide us with driving instructions. How hard could it be?

Finally, the big day arrived. After some false starts, we found the tour office on a narrow street in the center of Florence. We had arrived early and were the only ones in the tiny office space. A large travel poster on the wall behind the counter caught my eye: "ZOOM AROUND ON A VESPA!" it boldly proclaimed. The banner featured a picture of a young woman riding a shiny, mauve scooter. In place of a flowing headscarf, she wore a helmet, but she looked cool, just the same, in her oversized sunglasses.

"Are you here for one of our tours?" asked the clerk as she stepped out from a curtain covered doorway in the back of the office.

"Yes, we're here for the 10:00 Italian countryside tour and lunch," Ed affirmed.

"Wonderful! Names?" She checked us off the list. "Now I need your signatures on these waivers saying you release us from responsibility for any injuries you might incur."

We gave each other sideways glances but signed the waiver.

"Now, it's a good idea to buy insurance for the equipment. In case the Vespas are damaged, we will hold you responsible for repairs."

I heard Ann suck in her breath as our husbands pulled out their credit cards.

"Just a formality," the woman explained. "We hardly ever have any issues."

Perhaps Matt was right. Maybe we were in over our heads.

As the tour group assembled, I noted we were in the company of younger people. The guides ushered us into vans and we headed out. We soon left the congestion of Florence behind as we wound our way through the countryside. The narrow twisting roads were like what we experienced each morning as we left the villa and went into town.

"I don't think we'll be riding on *these* kinds of roads," I tried to reassure myself as I spoke to the young woman sitting next to me. "The brochure said we'd stay around the vineyard."

When we arrived at our destination, our host greeted us. The land and buildings had been in Francesco's family for generations and this was still a working vineyard. They'd added the Vespa tours and wine tasting business in recent years to offset operating costs. After a tour of the impressive wine cellar, Francesco led us to a gravel parking lot where orange traffic cones were arranged in a makeshift course.

"How many of you have driven a Vespa or motorcycle before?" he queried. Most of the crowd raised their hands, including Ed. I gave him a quick look.

"Put your hand down. The one time you rode a motorcycle you were fifteen, and you put it through the front window of your parents' house."

"But I know how to do this," he insisted.

One of the tour guides handed me a helmet and placed me in the beginners' line along with Ann and Scott, where we received our instructions.

"The first thing to know is you operate the machine from the handlebars. Brakes are here. Gas is here."

It seems simple, I thought to myself as I studied how the first group navigated around the cones. When my turn came, I straddled the purple machine as the cute, young Italian held the back of the seat for support. The Vespa was heavier than I'd expected and hard to balance.

"Now slowly give it some gas and when you start moving, take your feet off the ground," came the voice from behind.

As I pulled back on the handlebar, the Vespa lurched forward.

"Too much, too much, ease up, slow down." Now the guide was running behind me, his hand still on the back of my seat.

I was nervous and I couldn't remember which side of the handlebar was the brake and which was gas. At this slow speed, it was difficult to maintain my balance. We lurched and stopped, lurched and stopped until I'd made it halfway around the parking lot. I put my feet down and drug them in the gravel until the Vespa came to a stop. This wasn't like Audrey Hepburn at all. I'd had enough.

"Get... me... off... of this thing!" I panted.

"But Madame, you can do it. Let's go around once more."

"No, no. I'm done," I insisted. Looking up, I saw Ed careening off course. He was crashing through the olive grove with his guide dashing behind him.

Ann and Scott had fared little better. None of us passed the driving test. They gave us a choice of riding behind the Vespas in the support van or joining the wine tour and tasting that was already in progress. With our choice made, we watched the Vespas go zipping away (down the narrow, winding roads, mind you) and we trudged back to the villa to join the wine tasting session. There were only two others at the tasting table, a young couple on their honeymoon. Francesco set up four extra spots and listened as we told our sad tale. This was supposed to be our wild fling, our grand adventure, and we'd failed.

He poured a small amount of Chianti, the specialty of the region, into our glasses, then encouraged us to look at the color, swirl, smell the rich aroma, then sip, letting the ruby liquid slide down our throats. We were in no hurry as we would need to wait for the Vespa group to return before they served lunch. We chatted with the newlyweds and learned more about Francesco's family as we sipped our Chianti.

"So let me ask you, did you set out to have a good day today?" Francesco asked.

"Yes, we were looking forward to this," I sighed.

"And did you have a good day?" His next question took me by surprise. What could I say? No, the day didn't go as planned. I felt disappointed, embarrassed, and to be honest, *old*. Yet here I was sipping wine in a centuries-old villa with my husband and closest friends. We were surrounded by olive groves and vineyards on a beautiful October day. I set out to have an adventure and I'd had one. Besides, I was still in one piece and would have a hilarious story to tell my kids and grandchildren. I smiled.

"Yes...yes, we *are* having a good day!"

"Then I think you have no problem. Salute!" he said as he raised his glass. "La dolce vita."

And so it is. I realize now retirement has given me the gift of time and perspective. In the past few years, I'd broadened my horizons through travel. I'd had time to examine my life and prioritize how I want to spend my days. With my teaching career behind me, I can look back with pride on the work I'd done and look forward to what lies ahead. La dolce vita. The sweet life.

Part Four

New Horizons

*"Often when you think you're
at the end of something, you're
at the beginning of something else."*
~ Fred Rogers

Spike

Our retirement plans took us across the country. Most people think Ed and I moved to Arizona because it was what *we* wanted. The actual reason we moved to the desert is because that's where Spike would have wanted to live.

We adopted Spike in 2004 when his mother was dying. For many years his mother lived in a greenhouse on the upper floor of East High School in Columbus, Indiana, where Ed taught Biology. No one knew where she had originated from, and no one took much notice of her until she produced a huge stalk from her sturdy green center. She was a "century plant," an agave that flowers only once at the end of its long life. The mother plant was waning, but throughout her life she had produced countless shoots from her base to continue her lineage. The small greenhouse could no longer accommodate the large number of agaves as they stretched out their roots and grew. Staff members uprooted the orphans and placed them up for adoption.

I remember the day Ed brought the tiny plant home. He placed the pot on the kitchen counter along with his briefcase and lunchbox.

"Look what followed me home from school," he gushed.

I moved closer. "What is that?"

"It's an agave. The science department was giving them away. Can we keep him?"

I looked at the green plant with the succulent, tapered leaves. We knew nothing of raising agaves, but I was willing to give it a try. Ed named him Spike. He became our "ugly duckling," cute but awkward, nestled among the delicate Boston ferns and graceful philodendrons in a sunny corner of our Midwestern home.

Spike loved his new home. He soon outgrew his original pot, and the next one too. But Spike was living up to his name. The points on the ends of his leaves were growing into hazardous weapons. When he grew too large for his spot in the living room, we moved him to our master bathroom and placed him in the corner by the window. I think the move made him angry. One day he poked me in the behind when I was getting out of the tub. Now it was getting personal. I moved him from the bathroom to a spot under a window in our bedroom where he jabbed me when I was dusting or vacuuming. Finally, I had had enough.

"Do something with that plant of yours," I snapped at Ed.

"What do you mean?"

"It's dangerous. We have young grandchildren running around. It could poke out someone's eye."

He dismissed my concerns, but I no longer felt safe around Spike. I took matters into my own hands. After Ed left the house one day, I grabbed the kitchen shears and headed to the bedroom.

"Sorry, bud. But it has to be done."

One by one, I snipped off the menacing spikes. I carefully disposed of the clippings, thinking Ed wouldn't notice. For a while I thought I had gotten by with it. Then, a few days later, I heard a wail coming from the bedroom.

"What did you do to Spike? You *neutered* him!"

No amount of reasoning would calm my husband down. He remained mad at me for days.

Despite his neutered state, Spike sprouted three babies. We named them "Son of Spike," "Sugar and Spike," and "Mr. Spike" When they were old enough to survive on their own, we gave them away to friends.

Spike was never the same after the declawing episode and losing the babies. He turned pale and his leaves drooped. One warm spring day, out of desperation, we planted him outside in our herb garden. He perked up in the summer sun and was holding his own during the mild fall, but Indiana winters are unpredictable. He took a big hit after an unusual spell of cold, snow, and ice that year. In the spring he thawed out and dissolved into a heap of green-gray mush. We buried him under a pile of mulch and he became part of the garden soil. Ashes to ashes, mulch to mulch.

Meanwhile, our friends were having similar growing pains with Spike's children. Mr. Spike had become especially unruly. In the summer, his parents kept him in an enormous pot in their outdoor garden. During the winter months, they moved him into the basement. As the plant grew, the annual trek to and from the basement became an ordeal. Our friends donned coats, heavy gloves, and goggles to protect themselves as they lugged the pot up and down the narrow steps. When they heard we were moving to Arizona, they begged us to take Mr. Spike along and return him to the wild. We considered it, but by then he had gotten so large that it would have been impossible to get him in the backseat without impaling ourselves. Instead, we took one of his offspring, and named him after his grandfather, the original Spike.

The move from Indiana to Arizona was a monumental one for us. Our teaching careers were ending, and our children had moved away. We were leaving our Midwestern home and taking a chance on a new adventure. The moving van was already headed west. As we packed our car with the last of our belongings, we made a place for New Spike on the floor behind the driver's seat. The baby traveled well, requiring just a few sips of water during the three-day cross-country trip. He only tipped over once.

When we arrived in Arizona, we planted New Spike in our garden. He thrived in his natural habitat.

His leaves turned a rich, dark green, and he now stands four feet tall and four feet wide from tip to tip. New Spike has grown dangerously close to our walkway, but I dare not snip his spines. We've reached an agreement. If he doesn't play nice, I'll chop him down and make him into tequila. But really, I hope he lives long enough to produce a magnificent flower stalk and dies of natural causes like his great-grandmother before him. It is the way of the agave.

Along with Spike, Ed and I are thriving in our new environment. The warm sunshine and blue skies agree with us. We have many visitors in the winter and early spring months when Midwesterners droop and lose their color. When our friends and family comment on Spike, we tell the story of how a prickly plant led us to the desert. It's a good story. It was the right move.

Alone Together

After settling into our Arizona home, Ed and I enjoyed our new lives as a retired couple. We had a lot of time to spend together.

Lots...and...lots...of...time...together. It reminded me of one of my favorite children's stories, *Alone* from the *Frog and Toad* series by Arnold Lobel. In the story, Frog and Toad are best friends; they do everything together. One day Toad finds a sign on Frog's door saying he wants to be alone. Toad gets his feelings hurt. Why would Frog want to be by himself?

I'm with Frog on this one. My husband and I are very close. In fact, our relationship began as a college friendship. After spending nearly five decades as a married couple, we know each other well and enjoy each other's company. After we retired from teaching, I was excited to have lots of time to spend with Ed. We went on much-anticipated vacations to England and Italy. We visited our children and grandchildren and took day trips to explore the area around our new home in Tucson. Without a schedule, we no longer had to squeeze a year's worth of activity into breaks from school. Retirement seemed like a never-ending vacation.

 But in between all the fun activities, the days stretched out before me. I was losing myself in a fog of sameness and togetherness. I longed for something interesting to do.

Ed, a former high school science teacher, didn't feel the same way. Retiring several years before I did, he'd developed a routine that works for him. His interest in cooking benefits us both. He spends lots of time reading recipes and shopping for special ingredients and the perfect wine to accompany the dishes. His dinner parties are legendary and everyday meals are amazing. He putters with his telescope on clear Arizona nights. Although he detests yard work, he is very attached to his prized agave "Spike" and will go to great lengths to protect it in the winter. He's an avid reader. But not all of his activities are acceptable to me. I think he wastes too much time on the computer, watching TV, or staring at YouTube videos on his phone, and I tell him so. He says I'm nagging.

"How can you spend an entire morning playing on the computer? You need to get out of the house and *do* something," I'll gripe.

"I haven't been playing games on the computer *all* morning. Ed argues as he decides which card to play on the solitaire game on the screen.

"I can't understand how you are content to just *sit* there."

"Deb, I've worked since I was fourteen years old. I don't have to work anymore, and maybe I want to do something mindless for a while. I'm happy and I can't see why it bothers you. Besides, I don't tell you what to do, do I?"

He had a point. He seldom complained when I jumped from one project to the next or had lunch with friends. Even so, it seemed like we were spending too much time together. When we were busy raising our family and teaching, we used the dinner hour to reconnect and discuss the day's events. Table-talk included interesting news from high school or the current drama in my kindergarten class. Our children, Kelli and Matt, would chime in with bits about their day, or we'd jump up from the table to get someone to soccer or band practice. In retirement, we sometimes ate in silence, trying our best to come up with engaging conversations. There was no need to ask about each other's day. On most days, we were there. Together. Every minute.

I'd made friends during my three-year tenure as a teacher in Tucson and still enjoyed occasional meet-ups with my former teaching buddies. I'd taken an active role in my writer's forum and looked forward to their weekly gatherings. From what I could see, Ed's social group was me. Other than trips to the grocery store and outings that I planned, he seldom left the house. We were together too much, and I was going crazy. One day he took the car in for an oil change and

I had the place to myself for a few hours. Cranking up the volume on my favorite James Taylor CD, I sang along as I worked on a sewing project. Then, I danced into the kitchen and ate a spoonful of peanut butter right out of the jar, washing it down with a swig of white wine from the fridge. Ed doesn't appreciate the fine art of snacking. Sometimes a girl just needs a bit of freedom.

Another time, in search of some much needed girl-talk, I texted my friend:

Ed will be at the grocery store from 9-10:30 on Wednesday. RU available?

Nope. Dr. appt. What about Thursday morning?

OK...I'll sneak out of the house and call you from Starbucks.

LOL ... sounds like we're having an affair!

No, I wasn't having an affair. I didn't want a divorce. I just needed some space.

Ed and I didn't recite traditional vows at our wedding. In 1974 it was trendy to write your own, so we did. Wanting no part of "repeat after me," we planned to memorize our lines and surprise each other with our heartfelt sentiments. The minister advised against it, but we were adamant. It was our ceremony and we would let no one put words in our mouths.

At the right moment, Ed recited his vows perfectly. When it was my turn, I gazed into his eyes, opened my mouth, and then froze. My brain raced, but I couldn't remember the words I'd spent weeks composing. Awkward moments passed as I looked at the minister. He stood with an "I told you so" look on his face, unable to help me. There's a reason the bride and groom repeat their vows in short segments. Why did I think I could memorize an entire paragraph and recite it in front of hundreds of people on the biggest day of my life? Unwilling to make a total fool of myself, I made something up off the top of my head. Neither of us remembers what we pledged to each other that day. That may be the key to our marital longevity.

I see our decades-long path together as a series of stages: newlyweds, finishing college, starting careers, first-time parents, stay-at-home mom, both parents working, raising elementary-aged children, career changes, parenting teenagers (yikes!), empty nesters, becoming grandparents, and now, retirement. Each stage has brought its own joys and challenges. In order for our marriage to survive, it had to evolve. Just when we got comfortable with one stage, life threw us into the next. At those points we took a step back to reevaluate how things would work. Sometimes we planned it out like "Let's Make a Deal."

"Now that I'm working full time, I can't do all the shopping, laundry, and housework," I'd said.

"I can grocery shop if you make a list," Ed offered.

"Ok, I'll do the housecleaning, if you'll take laundry."

"Deal."

Other times, we weren't aware that we'd moved into a different stage until unrest set in. Hurt feelings, misunder-standings, tears, arguments, and silence clouded those days. But through it all, we maintained our relationship and our love. Whatever we'd vowed, or hadn't vowed, on our wedding day, we remain committed to each other.

We are continuing to adjust to this retirement stage. There have been some rocky parts. I still think he sits around the house too much and he can't figure out why I'm not content to stay put, but we're figuring it out bit by bit. We coexist in closer physical and emotional quarters than ever before, learning when to hold close, and when to spread our wings of independence. We hope to have many more years together. Yet, we know that most of our life is behind us. Someday, one of us will need to support the other, and the time will come when one will require the strength to fly solo.

For now, it's good to have someone to love who understands the balance of solitude and companionship. Arnold Lobel's Frog and Toad figured it out too. After spending some time by himself, Frog is glad to have Toad's company again. As they enjoyed a picnic lunch on the last page of the story, "they were two close friends sitting alone together."

Midnight Madness

I'm late. An enormous tote bag drags behind me as I trudge down the dark, narrow hallway. A sense of panic clouds my mind and I struggle to remember which room the meeting is in. I try several doors, but they are locked. My footsteps echo on the hard floor as I approach the end of the tunnel-like space. A sliver of light pushes under the closed door and I hear voices from within. My hand turns the doorknob and I inch open the door to reveal a meeting in progress. The conversation stops, and many eyes glare at me as I make my way to an empty seat and search through my cavernous bag for notes for my presentation. Deeper and deeper I dig, but come up empty-handed. "I'm, I'm sorry," I stammer, "but I can't seem to find what I am looking for." A voice coming from the head of the table barks, "Well, it looks as though Mrs. Van Deventer is NOT prepared."

Two years into retirement, my teacher anxiety dreams were less frequent, but still popped up from time to time. Showing up unprepared is a common theme. Most teachers I know report having similar night panics as daily stresses spill over into the subconscious mind, robbing them of much needed sleep.

It's the morning of the kindergarten field trip. Where are we going— the zoo? The apple orchard? The science museum? I'm not sure. Excitement runs high as my colleagues hand out name tags and arrange their chatty students into assigned groups. In horror, I realize I haven't made name tags or arranged my students into groups. To make matters worse, I've forgotten to get parent volunteers for the trip. While other teachers' students are lined up in organized, color-coded rows, mine are running all over the place. Somehow I get them on the bus and we arrive at our destination. As we exit the bus, a student asks, "Mrs. Van Deventer, where are our lunches?" We've left the lunches at school.

I woke myself up and ended this dream before it went any further. An out-of-control field trip is any teacher's worst nightmare. Like most educators, I was an excellent planner. It's not a brag; I didn't have a choice. Being ill-prepared for seven straight hours in a room full of energetic students is a *real* nightmare. Planning for field trips was the Holy Grail for teachers, the litmus test to see who was in control of her class—for all the world to see—and who was not. Over the years, I'd honed my organizational skills through trial and error. Ok... lots of errors. On one of my first field trips as a new teacher, I'd left behind a group of kindergarteners and their parent chaperones at the Indianapolis Zoo. (We got them back safe and sound... eventually.) By the time I had a few decades of teaching and more than fifty trips under my belt, I was a field trip guru and a color-coding queen. That's all behind me now. Why was my subconscious still planning field trips?

On another night, I'm back in the classroom:

I recognize this room. I used to teach here years ago. My first-grade classroom at Clifty Creek School comes into focus now and I see it is ready for the first day of school. My students will come soon. I stand at the door, eager to greet the arrivals. They look so cute with their shiny, new lunch boxes and fresh-from-the-store backpacks. "Welcome!" Find your nametag and take a seat," I say in my cheeriest teacher voice.

Students occupy every seat, and my first lesson is going well when the principal arrives at my door with a new student. "Jonathan has just enrolled, and we have placed him in your class. Please welcome him!" I smile, find a space at a table in the back of the room and help Jonathan settle in.

We've just resumed our lesson when the secretary comes to the door with two more students.

"Good morning," I say "Sit here in the book corner until we can find desks and chairs for you." Back to our lesson. But soon, the school nurse is at the door with more students. I give her a dirty look, plaster a smile on my face and make a space for them on the floor. Throughout the morning, more and more students arrive. By now there are first graders everywhere. First-graders are crammed into every available space. Those who don't have seats are running and jumping around the room. My well-prepared lesson plans are out the window as I try desperately to maintain control. A small girl appears at the doorway, lunchbox and backpack in hand. This is the last straw. "Oh no, you don't," I scream at her. "March yourself back up to the office and tell them THAT'S ENOUGH... I CAN'T TAKE ANY MORE KIDS!"

The poor, frightened girl dissolved into the background of my dream. This disturbed me. I would never have yelled at a student like that in real life. Sometimes I wanted to. There were times when I wasn't prepared for a meeting or a field trip. Times when a class or student was out of control. Times when I had to face an angry parent. Times when I wanted to lose my temper, lash out, scream, cry, or run away. I didn't. The emotions were genuine, but not allowed to show up between the school's arrival and dismissal bells. I would tamp them down, take a breath, and carry on. Sometimes my frustrations came out at home and I'd snap at Ed or the kids. My better self would go for a walk, practice my mindfulness lessons, or soak in a hot bath. But the underlying stress was ever present. Maybe that's why darker emotions and fears play out in dreams in the safety of slumber.

Recently I had a different sort of midnight message:

It looks like a party is going on. People have gathered to eat, drink, dance, and have a good time. I hear music. I notice I am flying above the crowd. The ceiling expands and fades away into the sky, allowing me to go higher and higher. My weightless self is enjoying newfound freedom. I try to show others how to do this amazing thing, but they don't seem to understand.

I awoke feeling wonderful. It was so different from my teacher-anxiety dreams. In doing some research, I learned a sensation of flying in one's dream can indicate a person feels out of control. That would fit in with some of the other dreams I'd been having. But reading more, I discovered it could also show the person is trying to gain a perspective on their true destiny or has suddenly come to a realization. The person is thinking outside the box and new opportunities may be on the horizon. I love this explanation. Forget the field trips, meetings, and crowded classrooms. I want to embrace this feeling of freedom.

One Step at a Time

Spring came to the desert, identified by a subtle difference in the air. The trail was lush with wildflowers showing off their brilliant shades of yellow, purple, coral, and white. A shallow stream ran across the path, the product of abundant winter snows high in the mountains. It was running ice cold and crystal clear, far from its mother snow. A line of delicate stepping stones invited hikers to cross one step at a time so as not to miss the music of the flowing water.

Almost three years had passed since my retirement. Slowing down was getting easier. It had taken longer than expected to get over feeling I had to rush through my days, cramming in as much as possible. Throughout my career, I'd gotten used to running on adrenaline, pushing myself to do more and more. Multitasking was a skill I had honed to perfection as I tried to keep my head above water. It was hard to break free of the hold it had over me.

The fast pace of my teaching life had become second nature. On most mornings, the alarm jarred me from a fitful sleep. I'd roll out of bed well before sunrise, make a potty stop, and zoom through my yoga routine on auto-pilot as I thought about the school day ahead of me. A nice warm shower would help wake me up. Then came the process of choosing what to wear. Professional dress was the expectation, comfort was the priority. Teaching young children is not a "sit at a desk" kind of profession and my clothes needed to be ready for action. To streamline my mornings, I'd kept my make-up routine and hair style simple. In the early years of my career, I had children at home. Getting Kelli and Matt up and going added an additional layer of activity as I helped them get ready for their day.

Adrenaline pumping, I arrived at school prepared to greet twenty-five to thirty energetic kinder-garteners, first graders or, later in my career, fourth graders. At the end of a long day of teaching, there were teacher meetings, staff development sessions, or parent conferences to attend. I'd bring home anything that didn't get finished and often woke in the middle of the night going through lesson plans in my head. Done. Click. Repeat. For thirty-seven years.

Looking back through the lens of time, I remember those early years of teaching to be less hectic than my later years were. I was younger then, which explains part of it. Yet, I also saw the demands on educators escalate through the years. Standards increased and the pace quickened as administrators and lawmakers added more and more to the curriculum. Class sizes grew and it became harder to meet the diverse needs of my students. Attempting to keep up, I perused educational websites seeking to do more in less time. "Too Many Tasks... Not Enough Day" and "Take Control of Your Time" the articles cried out. Some teachers were better at time management than others. There was always a Mrs. X down the hall that made it look easy, and I wished I was more like her. But day after day, year after year, the frantic pace took its toll. Even on Mrs. X. Studies show that multitasking is not healthy or beneficial to us. Some research says bombarding our brain with too much at once can diminish productivity and lead to mental exhaustion. Mental exhaustion—that's what is etched on the faces of educators gathered for a faculty meeting at the end of an already long day.

During my last year, teachers at my school chose what staff development course they wanted to pursue. We could sign up for mindfulness training (a hot new topic in education) or curriculum writing. *Everyone will choose mindfulness training,* I thought. *Who would want to spend their afternoon writing curriculum?* It surprised me to discover my teammates and many others did just that. I think they were afraid that "mindfulness" sounded like strange voodoo magic, or perhaps they decided if they had to write a curriculum anyway, they might as well get it done in the time provided. So as the professional development sessions began after school, my friends grabbed their teacher manuals and trotted off to their class down the hall. I joined my group in the library.

We pushed the tables aside and arranged a circle of chairs Kum-Ba-Yah style. I wasn't sure what to expect, but at least I could sit down and rest.

"Hi! Welcome! Sign in please and pick up a notebook and journal," directed a soft-spoken young man with wire-rimmed glasses and a kind face. He walked around on quiet, comfortable shoes, his long dreadlocks neatly pulled back in a headscarf. He appeared to be a mindful sort of guy.

"Take your seats and we'll get started." Being the excellent role models we were, we gathered our supplies and found seats. The session began with a typical ice breaker.

"So introduce yourself and tell us why you focused on mindfulness for your professional development this year."

"I showed up for the snacks, but I don't see any."

"I thought it might be easier than the alternative."

"The library is close to my room. I was too exhausted to walk down the hall."

All legitimate answers. We giggled. Then one small voice spoke up.

"I came because I'm tired of being pulled in many directions. I'm tired of late nights and early mornings. I'm tired of not being able to finish anything. I'm tired of multitasking. I'm tired. That's it... I'm tired."

It could have been me. It could have been any of us. We nodded in agreement.

"Then let's get started."

And so we did. At first we practiced sitting with our minds and bodies still. Sounds simple, but for a room full of folks who had been racing around all day, maybe even chasing the clock their entire lives, it was incredibly difficult.

"Close your eyes," our guide intoned. "Breathe in, breathe out. Focus on your breath. If your mind wanders, bring it back to the breath..."

I closed my eyes and tried to relax my tight shoulders.

This is nice... so peaceful... quiet at last... breathe in... breathe out... I could get used to this... the school orchestra is starting practice next door...bless their hearts, you can tell they are beginners... block it out... focus... I'm kind of hungry... too bad there are no snacks... I wonder what we are having for dinner?...breathe in...out...focus on the breath... my butt's asleep... how long have we been sitting here?...I need to run off the math test for tomorrow...in... out... does Barb still have her eyes closed?...back to the breath, back to the breath! What's wrong with me? Keep breathing...in...out.. peek at my watch...three minutes...it's only been three minutes?!

And so it went, month by month, step by step, we learned how to untangle our minds. It was wonderful. Like voodoo magic without sticking pins in dolls. I came out of those sessions relaxed and refreshed. But, even though I was working on techniques to incorporate mindful living in my personal and professional life, it was impossible to keep it up on a day-to-day, minute-by-minute basis. Like anything else, it takes time and a commitment to practice. I was motivated but couldn't dim the clatter of my busy life.

After I'd retired, it had taken me several years to learn to enjoy life at a different pace. I had gotten so used to running on adrenaline and schedules that I struggled at first with what to do with myself. For a while my unstructured days frightened me and I tried to fill them up—panicked that I was wasting time. Determined to work through it, I resisted the urge to replace one busy life for another. I needed space to readjust, rest, and recharge the batteries that would fuel me through this next phase of my life. Like an adrenaline junkie in rehab, I was making progress one step at a time.

On that spring day, my office was the foothills of the Catalina Mountains, and I was in charge of my own agenda. I started to cross the dainty mountain stream but was drawn to stop. The sound of the water running over the stones was music enough to quiet my mind, and I stood drinking in the delicious melody. At that moment, my schedule was empty, but my life was full. I sat in the soft grass, pulled out my notebook and captured thoughts that would evolve into one of my first poems, *Stream Song*.

A shallow stream
runs through the lush desert valley,
newborn of the abundant winter
in the Catalina Mountains.

Running ice cold far from Mother Snow,
its crystal-clear voice rings out
in playful babbles
as it toddles along.

Stepping stones lie across the stream,
bidding travelers to navigate
one timid step at a time,

slowly,
quietly,

so as not to miss the gift
of the baby stream's song.

Write Now

Sunlight tiptoes through the slats in the window blinds, nudging me awake. The days are lengthening; my biological clock adjusts itself to the rhythm of daylight and darkness. This morning's yoga session is leisurely; breakfast and a walk follow. After showering, I put on comfy leggings and a soft tunic top. Shoes are optional. The tea kettle signals that my morning brew is ready. I make my way to my office/studio, open my journal and greet... a blank page. There it is, taunting me.

You have no plans.
What are you going to do today, this week, this year, huh?
Where's your schedule?
Do you even know how to operate without lesson plans?
People expect you to keep busy. Busy is good.

Early in retirement, the empty page intimidated me. After spending most of my life as a student or a professional woman, I found myself addicted to schedules, plans, and the adrenaline that fueled my busy days. For decades, I'd get up, rush through my morning routine, and speed off to school. Once there, my day was planned to the minute and packed with activity. Teaching had been a major part of my world. I'd worked hard to succeed and had been passionate about my profession. Now what? How would I fill the void? Where do I begin?

I journaled. Putting words on pages each morning gave form to my random and disjointed thoughts. Over time, writing helped me through the grieving process so I could come to terms with retirement. Up to this point, I'd followed a predictable path: college, marriage, children, and career. Even my retirement was predictable, though I'd postponed it compared to many. For the first time in a long while I asked myself, "What do *you* want to do?" Family, friends, and travel would be important. I also explored my creative self with the help of books such as *The Artist's Way* by Julia Cameron and *The Creative Habit* by Twyla Tharp. It took a while, but as the stress left my body, I no longer feared the void. I realized that the blank page, free of rigid plans and expectations, was my ticket to a full life.

Eager to explore my artistic nature, I discovered a writer's forum sponsored by the local library. Here I found writers, at all levels of expertise, who gathered twice a month to share their latest works. My first attempt at reading one of my stories aloud reminded me of anxious times when my six-year-old self had to read aloud in Mrs. Clarisey's first grade class. Though I'd long gotten over my fear of public speaking, as I read in front of the forum that day, my hands shook and I stumbled over words. When I finished my selection, I avoided eye contact and shoved my papers back into my notebook. To my surprise, the group smiled and applauded. Even though they did this for each reader, it was the encouragement I needed. From that moment on, the writer's forum became a regular part of my weekly routine.

In between scheduled meetings at the library, many gathered at a local coffee shop. Friendships developed as we discussed our latest writing projects, shared insights, and gave each other support. Up until now, I'd kept my writing to myself. Here I found my tribe—a gathering of like-minded folks who understood what it meant to be a writer.

When asked to join a small critique group, I jumped at the chance. The five of us continue to meet, sharing our writing and getting feedback. In the company of writing friends, it's safe to take chances with my work. They push me to dig deeper to find my voice as a writer. I welcome the encouragement, but more importantly, giving and receiving honest critiques improves my writing. This is my chance to bloom. I have plenty of time, a supportive group of friends, and a renewed surge of creative energy.

I feel fortunate to have the opportunity for this encore "career." Like teaching, passion drives my writing, but I am working on my own terms this time. I'm on my own time-table, following my own path. I see myself as a storyteller, focusing on small moments others can identify with. Those first stories focused on teaching and retirement, but adventures with friends and family or personal observations also inspire me. Through writing, my vision expands as I view the world through an artist's eye.

So this is where I am on my life's journey. Honoring my past as an educator, exploring my future as a writer. Blessed with family, friends, and stories to tell. This is me. Write now.

The Breadcrumb Trail

Another school year is coming to a close and soon teachers will gather for the annual end-of-the-year luncheon. One of my colleagues is retiring this year and will make her way to the front of the cafeteria to be honored. I was in her shoes three years ago. It seems like yesterday, yet it feels like a lifetime has passed. From the podium she will deliver an eloquent speech or perhaps, like I did, her throat will choke with emotion, unable to say what is in her heart. What she may not yet understand is that she is standing on the edge of the rest of her life.

During the first weeks of my retirement, I was searching for a guidebook of instructions to help me navigate this vast new, open territory. I never found the breadcrumb trail to follow. Instead, I found my own way through one step at a time. My newly retired friend will find her path too, in her own way and own time, as she should. A breadcrumb trail is merely a suggestion, a temporary path laid down by someone who has gone before. Birds may well devour it before the traveler even gets there. And yet, if I could speak at my friend's luncheon, here is the breadcrumb trail I would offer.

***

Even though you are looking forward to this milestone, prepare yourself for some unexpected emotions. Retirement marks the end of an era and you will experience a loss. A loss of friends, a loss of routine and structure, a loss of professional purpose, a loss or reduction in income. This emotional roller coaster derailed me. Before I made it back to the classroom after my retirement luncheon, I was sitting on the sidewalk sobbing into my cake. No one warns you about this when you are filling out the mountain of paperwork. There is no Retirement 101 course. Allow yourself the time to grieve as you would with any other type of loss. It has taken me several years. You may adjust more quickly or you may need more time than I did, but be forewarned, it will be a major change.

Celebrate! I know you will have a nice get together in your honor at the school. Maybe your friends and colleagues will take you out for dinner or happy hour. Perhaps your school district will mark your years of service with recognition of some sort or your family will throw a party in your honor. When my husband Ed retired from high school, his colleagues put together a hilarious "Celebrity Roast" for him. Most likely, there will not be a gold watch with your name engraved on it or a large bonus check. That's OK, no one wears watches anymore anyway, although the bonus check would be nice. But do *something* to mark this milestone in your life. Whether you have worked for five, twenty-five, or thirty-seven years, retirement is a **Big Deal**! Do something monumental: take a trip, throw yourself a party. One person I know invited his friends and family to a backyard shindig featuring the band he played in. It needn't be a big, elaborate, expensive affair. I ended up putting together an inexpensive, last minute "dinner cruise" around the local lake on a pontoon boat with my family. We had a blast! I took lots of pictures and made a photo book to remember the occasion. My point is, mark the occasion in a way that is meaningful to you. You deserve it, and it will help you put closure on a big part of your life.

Honor your past. I went back and visited each of the buildings that were part of my teaching career. They were still standing, and all but one are still being used as schools, which helped to make me feel like I wasn't an old geezer. My trip down memory lane occurred during the summer when the schools weren't in session, but I took pictures of each building. Once I was back home, I put together a small photo album. As I was jotting down memories, I realized each school represented an era or time frame in my life. There were opportunities to make friends, work with talented professionals, and interact with countless students and families. I witnessed an impressive array of educational movements from 1970 to 2018 and was proud of my contributions. Even if you aren't able to visit your teaching past physically, take some time to visit it emotionally. You have a lot to be proud of!

So honor your past, but don't live there. Get ready for the rest of your life. You have time now to do what you want to do. Lots of unstructured time. This can be amazing, but it can also be daunting. At first I was anxious and stressed because I had nothing to be stressed out about. There were boring days, but I set aside a year where I resisted the temptation to sign up for anything that would lock me into a schedule. There were opportunities to substitute, teach or volunteer at a school, but frankly, that part of me was depleted, and I needed to allow myself time to recharge. Some people are afraid to retire because they can't imagine how they would fill their time. I get it. That, in part, was why I stretched out my teaching career for an extra three years. In retirement, interests I'd put on the back burner for many years emerged. Find your passion. Meet new people. Travel. Go for it!

This next breadcrumb is a little hard to swallow. I hesitate to even bring it up, but you need to know that retirement is not the pot of gold at the end of the rainbow. First, there is no gold (you probably already figured that out), but also, being retired doesn't exempt you from life. You will still face the challenges of day-to-day living: health scares, family squabbles, financial concerns, closet clutter, aches and pains, midriff bulge... The Retirement Fairy Godmother does not wave her magic wand and turn you into a new person; you will still be you.

But that is the best part. You will still be *you*. The fact that you have survived, even thrived, in the world of education, and made it out in one piece is a testament to the kind of person you are. You are creative, resilient, hardworking, resourceful, positive-thinking, a problem solver, and just a bit crazy. These are the qualities that will carry you through this next stage of your life. You are in charge from here on out and you will be amazing.

Now go out and buy yourself a new box of crayons. Splurge and get the ninety-six pack with wild, unique colors and sparkles. Oh, and be sure the box has the crayon sharpener on the back. You are going to be coloring in a whole new world!

Epilogue
The Beginning

I finished sewing the last button on my latest creation. The bright yellow, white, and gray cotton had been in my fabric stash for years. The geometric print reminded me of something you might see in a 1950s kitchen. Maybe I intended it to be an apron or curtains. It wanted to be a skirt. The high-waisted, gathered, slightly above-the-knee garment wasn't my usual style. It seemed retro and modern at the same time. That's why I liked it. I pulled it on over a white tee shirt and fastened the buttons around my waist.

I glanced in the mirror. There was no doubt that I was aging. I'd quit coloring my hair when I left teaching; the silver strands in my short pixie cut matched the gray in my new skirt. Bifocal glasses now replaced my contact lenses. A few more wrinkles, age spots, and sags appeared on my face. Yet, I must say that my life out of the classroom agreed with me. I was older and wiser. At the same time, I felt energetic and young. Retro and modern, like my skirt.

I slipped on a pair of black sandals, grabbed my purse, and checked my tote bag to make sure I had what I needed for my meeting.

"See you about lunch time," I called to Ed as I headed for the door.

The traffic light flashed red as I approached the turn lane at the intersection of Oracle and Ina. I braked suddenly, annoyed I hadn't been able to sneak through. I planned to meet some friends at the local coffee shop and was running late. My eyes darted to the rearview mirror, relieved that the car behind me had stopped. Tucson drivers have a tendency to speed through red lights, and I feared I might get rear-ended.

I glimpsed the driver. Her fluffy gray hair, coiffed into an old lady style, was shining in the bright sunlight like a silver halo around her plump face. I categorized the lady as a nice grandmotherly type, probably on her way to the grocery store. Beige, gray, predictable, boring. Is that what people think when they see me? There must be more.

Still stopped at the traffic light, I stole another glance at the woman in the car behind me and caught a glimpse of red lipstick. The bright red lips slashed through my original perceptions of this woman. She had taken the time to put on flashy lipstick. Perhaps she's not going to the grocery store after all. An interesting character was emerging.

The turn arrow would flash any second now, but I was curious. I needed more information. A flick of my eyes to the mirror revealed the red-lipped, silver-haired woman wore oversized, dark sunglasses and exaggerated hoop earrings. I liked her style.

Green arrow. Time to move. As I made the turn onto Ina, the Mini Cooper followed close behind until we rounded the corner, then raced by me in the left-hand lane. That's when I noticed the two black rally stripes running from the hood, across the top and down the back, turning the sensible beige vehicle into a mini race car. I caught a blur of black-and-white checkered wing mirrors as she sped up, widening the gap between us. Where was she going in such a hurry? An important business meeting? A secret rendezvous? I was on the trail of a story.

She was getting away! I knew what I had to do. I pulled into the parking lot of the coffee shop and lurched to a stop. My hand searched in my tote bag until I found the metal spiral of my notebook. Taking a pen from the cup holder on the console, I captured this character on paper: silver-halo hair, red lips, sunglasses, hoops, racing stripes, checkered wings flying past.

The clock on the dash showed that I was fifteen minutes late for my meeting, but I wasn't concerned. My friends would understand. After I'd finished my notes, I put my journal back into my tote bag and made my way to the cafe. At the counter, I ordered a latte.

"How's your morning going?" the barista asked.

"Good! I'm meeting with my group today." I motioned to the bunch gathered with notebooks and pens at our usual spot by the windows.

"So, you're a writer?"

Her question took me by surprise. Since retiring, I'd been working on my writing. Several of my stories and poems appeared in the writers' forum anthologies, and a local magazine had published two of my pieces. I'd recently started a blog. Even so, I'd been hesitant to identify myself as a writer. Was I confident enough to do so now? I glanced back at my friends huddled together, already discussing each other's works. They'd saved a spot for me.

"Yes. Yes, I *am* a writer," I affirmed.

And that's just the beginning...

Acknowledgements

Thanks to everyone who helped me along this journey. This work could not have been accomplished without the support and encouragement of the Oro Valley Writers Forum. Special thanks to Brad, Devi, Karen, David, and Elizabeth for challenging me to bring forth my best over cups of coffee, tea, and lunch. You guys are the best.

And with deepest appreciation for my husband Ed for his love, support and encouragement through all our moments. Here's to more adventures to come.

The story *Up in the Air, A Traveler's Tale in Four Parts* first appeared in *Desert Muses, Oro Valley Writers Forum Anthology II*

And the story of *Spike*, the agave who moved us to Arizona, first appeared in the January 2021 edition of *Desert Leaf* magazine.

About the Author

Debra VanDeventer is a former educator who now channels her creative energies into writing. Her style can best be described as creative nonfiction as small moments bloom into short stories and poems. She is an active member of the Oro Valley Writers Forum and has published works in both editions of their anthologies, *Monsoon Madness* and *Desert Muses.*In addition, her stories have appeared in *The Desert Leaf* magazine.

Originally from Indiana, Debra has two children and three grandchildren. Along with her husband Ed, she resides in Arizona where life in the desert never ceases to amaze and inspire her. To learn more, visit her blog at **seamslikeastory.com**

Made in the USA
Middletown, DE
18 June 2022